A Savage Culture

A Savage Culture
Racism – a black British view
Remi Kapo

QUARTET BOOKS
LONDON   MELBOURNE   NEW YORK

First published by Quartet Books Limited 1981
A member of the Namara Group
27/29 Goodge Street, London W1P 1FD

Copyright © 1981 by Remi Kapo

ISBN 0 7043 2302 8

Typeset by King's English Typesetters Limited, Cambridge
and printed in Great Britain by
King's English Bookprinters Limited, Leeds, Yorkshire

To the black and Asian peoples who died in the fires of New Cross and Southall. To those whites who have also died for the same cause. To Malcolm X whose death achieved his aim and ours. To Nelson Mandela whose very life and continued existence reinforces the flame of Human Rights into a permanent monument of resistance. And finally, to those young Britons who have not yet made up their minds.

Contents

Preface	xiii
1 An African Dream	1
2 Rule Britannia	17
3 A Savage Culture	37
4 On the Brink	65
5 The Order Architects	87
6 In Cold Storage	107
7 Prospects	127

Acknowledgements

I wish to acknowledge my mother and father for the solid effort they made for me. They were the people whose African Dream, in essence, powered the basis of my ideas. To Margo Reid, who has humanity completely covered with compassion. A kindred spirit across the colour line. Gary Grant, a rebel for the same cause of Human Rights, and a brother. All those people at Quartet Books who supported me during the writing and publication of this book. Dee Wells, Ivor French, 'remember what we asked the years to do with our lives?' Priscilla and John McBride, Shokat Babul, Chenhamo C. Chimutengwende, Roy Hiscock, in Rock Road, a friend. Jill Warner, who kindly mowed a green lawn of controversy. Cecil Gutzmore, for his untiring support of black youth. To Joyce and Alex Pascall, the other branch of an African tree. To Jeannette de Haas, a sister, a spirit of enormous ability who has my respect. This list would not be complete without acknowledging the influence of C.L.R. James, Kwame Nkrumah and Walter Rodney.

The author and publishers would like to thank the following for permission to reproduce material quoted in this book:

Oxford University Press for lines from 'Epilogue' from *Rights of Passage* by Edward Kamau Brathwaite. Copyright © Oxford University Press 1967

Monthly Review Press for *The Black Man's Burden* by E. D. Morel

Jan Morris for extracts from *Pax Britannica, Heaven's Command* and *Farewell Trumpets*

Leicester University Press for *Colour, Class and the Victorians* by Douglas A. Lorimer

War on Want for *Now You Do Know* by John Downing and an extract from Bishop Colin O'Brien Winter's foreword; and for *From Massacres to Mining* by Janine Roberts

New Society for 'It couldn't Happen Here' and 'Dagenham's Way With Colour' by Remi Kapo. Copyright ©*New Society* 1977

New Statesman for 'Tolerated Guests' by Remi Kapo

George Allen and Unwin Publishers Limited for *Power* by Bertrand Russell

Penguin Books Limited for *Beyond the Limits of the Law* by Tom Bowden, published by Pelican Books 1978

Should you

Shatter the door
and walk
in the morning
fully aware

of the future
to come?
there is no
turning back

Rights of Passage, Edward Kamau Brathwaite

Preface

In 1980/81 street disturbances in Bristol, Brixton, Southall and Liverpool shocked the nation. Britain accidentally discovered that the customary gospel of cutting close to the edge without going down was impossible. Running out of luck, it was a psychic bring-down. For the sad, seductive bitter-sweet suspicion of some, of a possible racial struggle, finally erupted and stoned the Soul. We were all straightened out by the stretching, stark reality, that at the edge of any racial precipice is a very long drop. The Old Deal of righteously 'riding out a storm', has been hammered into skull-dragging perspective; sizzling in the bulletin, is the fact that Britain is squatting on a permanent hornet's nest of colour/class reaction. But, the essence, the heart of the matter is: there is no Quality Time for some in the political and social justice of Britain.

Nevertheless, there have been gentle warnings chalked on the wall in a number of publications, which should have ripped down the mask of pretence that no other reality exists in present-day Britain. They were mostly presented by whites, some of whom were making a living 'taking care of business'; but all had attempted to present the black or Asian reality. Additionally, if sincerity is a foundation, it is definitely impossible to write about *any* injustice with a muffled pen; for outrage demands the hot ink of belief, for clarity. This book presents a black British view.

However, there are those, black, brown and white alike, who passionately care, and have spoken out against racial inequality only to be coldly dismissed by the silence of others. And silence is the acceptable lover of prejudice. Silence is the mouthpiece for injustice.

The rigor mortis reliance on the ability to control any racial confrontation through the possible use of naked power, or the rusty creed of 'repatriation' urged by reckless advocates, in my view, are giant miscalculations. In Britain, the biting use of naked power will most probably dominate any such racial protest. But at what cost? For humanity will weep. And why should anybody weep?

I was raised in Britain to believe in the moral reasonings of the democratic ideal. And growing through the scales of time, I learned the harsh reality that that ideal was and is immorally practised in the question of race. Therefore, black and Asian racial philosophy springs from the continual criticism of white race beliefs. But timing politics is an art. Timing racial politics requires inspiration, and moral courage to carry out an equitable solution.

· The principle forming the basis for belief in Human Rights is the single most important ideal for mankind, universally. It is in this ideal I believe.

Remi Kapo
London, August 1981

1
An African Dream

Nineteen fifty-three was a decisive year for the Constitution of the United Kingdom: Queen Elizabeth II was crowned at Westminster Abbey. It was that same Constitution which held sway over the trial and conviction of Jomo Kenyatta and five other Kikuyu leaders for organizing Mau Mau. It was also an important year for me, because on 30 August 1953, accompanied by my father, I arrived aboard the M/V *Apapa* at Tilbury Docks to begin an English education. I was seven.

The significance attached to Her new Majesty was completely lost on me, although it was something I was to question later. But the plight of Kenyatta was quite different. Despite my inability to comprehend the nature of his adversity, his black face on a newspaper page aroused a racial reflex in me.

Kenyatta was in trouble. This I gleaned from conversations I overheard between my father and other passengers on the long voyage out of Apapa, Lagos, Nigeria. The added shipboard speculation that he might be executed as well increased my sympathy.

I was born into a colonized Nigeria. I had heard pronouncements of 'death by hanging' of blacks by the white authorities many times before. This threat to Kenyatta's life was different.

The attitude of my father and his friends was one of dismay and the note of urgency in their voices added excitement. Their collective frame of mind, one of intensifying frustration and fear, was emphasized by many whispered conversations and continual checking at the cabin door. Outside on deck, fearing eavesdroppers, wary glances were thrown over-the-shoulder before anything was said.

From the little I could understand I managed to grasp that a wind of change was blowing across Africa, that there were certain 'natives' who did not like the way the whites were running affairs in their countries, that those natives thought it was high time for whites to hand back to them the government of their respective countries; and that there were blacks who were quite prepared to force the whites to hand over everything. Kenyatta, they said, was one such man.

By this time the ship-bound comrades were thinking of themselves as partners in a well-organized African guerrilla unit, permanently on call to any spot in Africa where whites were refusing to hand over power. They were not about to concede to the treasonous nature of their discussions, mainly because of the inspiration of Kenyatta, a black like themselves, who intended to free his people from the grasp of the British Empire. The fight for Independence was becoming a highly contagious colonial fever and my father and his fellow-travellers who obviously resented the theft of their land and the racist nature of British Administration, also wanted out. In a besieged garrison every sentinel is a potential deserter. From what I understood, the British saw themselves as the garrison and the blacks as the deserters. Hence, what the authorities were bound to see as 'seditious conversations' were conducted mostly in our cabin at night, in low tones, in our language, Yoruba.

Such was my introduction to the pernicious use of racial difference and the naked realities of African politics. I did not see it that clearly at the time, still less did I realize its meaning as I sailed into the United Kingdom.

Nigerian parents in the fifties were obsessed by educational ambitions for their children. The energies and hopes of a people reacting to the prospect of Independence were manifested in a ferocious competition to educate the next generation.

India, for so long a jewel in Britain's crown, became the Joan of Arc of colonized peoples. Her recently won self-emancipation fired the lust for freedom in other colonies. In the minds of most Nigerians who felt soured by their history, there was a craving to make news. For them the Empire was a confusing mixture of exploitation, inefficiency, brutality and greed. If it could not be exported for Britannic gain, then Britain was not interested, and many things were left under- and undeveloped. Education was one of them.

To have a son at King's College, Ibadan, twenty miles north of Lagos, was a family distinction. The rivalry for places at such fee-paying institutions was so fierce that family feuds shook neighbourhoods and parted life-long friends. With such high stakes some parents were suspected of poisoning others' children. They dreamed of their offspring as cabinet ministers, captains of industry and commerce, lawyers and so on, as well as guarantees of their own future security. Failure meant that their thwarted ambitions were bestowed on the children, occasionally with horrifying effects. Beatings meted out by success-oriented parents sometimes resulted in hospitalization, if they were lucky enough to live near one of the few infirmaries. At school, minor offences, such as lateness and incorrect uniform, invariably led to expulsion, the cause of which may have been the deliberate tactic of a 'friend', who had delayed a school-bound child, or persistently reported him for unruly behaviour. The 'friend's' child, it was hoped, would fill the vacancy.

Out of this crusade grew another mania. Educating children at English boarding-schools. Parents devoured the enticing advertisements: a child who had been educated in Britain fetched a higher premium on returning; he would not only possess an English qualification, but would also dress like an Englishman and, to crown it all, talk like one. Evening discussions would find many parents glowing with ambitious pride, dreaming of Reunion Day at Apapa Wharf where they would meet their extended babies, with their surname on a degree certificate. Those port scenes were frantic and filled with frightening expectations. Yesterday's dreams when realized could lead the aspirants on the road

3

either to becoming just another casualty of political ambition – especially when they discovered that their allegiance to nationalism was stronger than their allegiance to the Church – through a *coup d'état* and execution, or to success and eminence.

Someone had sold the idea of a boarding-school in St Leonard's, Sussex, England, to my father. On this school his sights were set and his hopes founded. Ledsham Court School became my destination. After being told about my conscripted journey, passports, packing luggage, packing me – by this time my reluctance to leave my mother and everything I had ever known was becoming a problem – vaccinations and tickets were completed in a blur. And such were the methods of the savage Afro/British education market, that I found myself on the road to the docks on the way to obey my father's decree, to become a barrister. Time was to be anaesthetized, for the farewells at Apapa Wharf were accomplished in the full expectation that I would, literally, return tomorrow, qualified.

Landing in England, the 'mother country', whose streets I had been told reassuringly were paved with gold, produced in me an overwhelming emotion. I was stunned. I felt parts of me trembling, my body chemistry altered and I was revitalized. I goggled at the sea of faces and was frightened by its whiteness, I felt myself drowning in the intensity of its stare. Confused and dazzled by the fug of a thousand cars, the sights, sounds and smells of an alien country, we arrived at a hotel in Earls Court, London. The image of Ibadan, my home town in Nigeria, was already beginning to drop out of my news.

Next day, Ledsham Court School, through the impending visit from my new headmistress, loomed into my present. The exchange was made with me as the currency. I travelled down to Sussex with my new guardian and my father returned to Nigeria, alone. Such was the pain, the shock, the surprise and the magic of my English homecoming.

The school was a masterpiece. A beautiful mansion with a facade of woven ivy, set in acres of green placid fields and woodland. A boulevard-wide tarred oval drive with a rhododendron bush dead centre completed the impressive frontage. My vision increased as we entered a gargantuan assembly hall with a harlequin-tiled floor and a gallery half-way up the walls, leaving me gazing up through a glass roof to the sky above. From an African landscape to this, I was astonished. Pride died and I crumbled, as memories of Ibadan flooded back. Tears were wiped away, army fashion, as I was prepared for lunch.

Salad was for lunch but a plateful of lettuce was not for me. I was dragged out of the dining-room in front of the entire school, pulled along the corridor to the hall and whacked. I was filled with dread, it was only my first day, what would the rest be like? This ceremony completed, I was hauled back in. The stares, whispers and murmurs which heralded my initial entrance to the dining-room, increased in volume on my return, stiffening my resolve. I still refused to eat the lettuce and was promptly banished to my room.

Later that afternoon I was again presented to the lettuce, to no avail. On closer inquiry by members of the staff who finally decided that it might be time to ask me why I would not eat what they thought was good for me, I revealed that in my country only animals ate raw vegetables. They reluctantly relented. But the punishment of being smacked by hand was followed very quickly by exercise books across my face, the ruler's edge on my knuckles, and the ultimate sanction, the cane.

In these tortures, I was treated no differently from any other member of the co-educational school, except perhaps in that the frequency of these punishments was peculiar to me. The reaction of the school to my repetitive visits to the Headmistress's study for punishment set the racial trend. Golliwog in Enid Blyton's Noddy books came to life in the guise of 'that naughty black boy from Africa'. The jungle stereotype was complete.

Despite the shock of my entry into this school, I had my moments: summer nights which seemed to last for ever; early evenings when a few of us would play down by The Rocks endlessly, without a care in the world; days of nature study, near a hide-out by the pond, where a single dragonfly with its long brilliant body and large wings would hold me spellbound and where waterboatmen careened across the mirrored surface, capturing my spirit, while the gentle seduction of the teacher's voice opened up a world seemingly uninterrupted by time. These were

5

beautiful and memorable moments.

On the negative side of the school curriculum, however, were history, geography, mathematics and English. In history I was taught how magnificent the British Empire was, how lucky I was to be part of it and how the English had conquered half the world. Being the only black in the school, I was that half. In geography, I learned just how dark Africa was. Maths began as no problem, but it became one through a lack of encouragement and fulfilled the myth of my academic inability. But English was the *pièce de résistance*. It went something like this. Spoken English and Civilization were synonymous. Africa was uncivilized and I was an African. So it was decided to begin the civilizing process with me. I would speak perfect English and elocution was drafted in. My accent today stands as a tribute to their thoroughness.

Due to a family crisis, I had to leave this school. The Headmistress and I said goodbye with tears in our eyes. The goodbyes were sad and sudden. I was heartbroken, for it felt as if I was leaving home again. Someone accompanied me to my next boarding-school in Kent, and somebody else to my next in Surrey, all in descending order of fees.

It was 1958 and the last step on my spiral staircase, covering the British social and educational spectrum, was Beechholme, and this one was free. On the list of other activities, of which there were many, was a necessary course of study familiarly termed street sense. Beechholme was an institution for orphans, deserted children and children of parents with 'difficulties'. It was the property of and administrated by the old London County Council. At the age of twelve, after five years in Britain, my feet finally touched the ground.

Beechholme was a place of disgrace. The Public Eyes who comfortably inhabited the nearby villages of Nork, Banstead, Banstead Village and Belmont, used Beechholme as a slur. To make the gulf absolute, we were from The Home. That meant we were either social lepers or a bunch of thieves. Outside its walls, to claim residence of a respectable neighbourhood was natural.

In Beechholme, the pollution of social disgrace penetrated the mentality. Scorn guarded its gates avidly like a leech. The inmates, now devalued in social terms, struggled with hope, as an idea, particularly if they were black. It was a place to steal away from and snuff from the memory as a bizarre, embarrassing dream. It never happened. The concrete aggression of the general public blew out any hope of contact. There was no let-up. I found this to be the crushing reality of English life, that it can so destabilize an individual, flattening his ego, that he soon knows his place. In Beechholme this cut-rate resignation was refreshed by the monotony of discouragement and lack of interest from the staff, and leaden hours of boredom. Most insiders were crushed by their sentence. But some damaged beings climbed above their abasement with rebellion or a craving for getting out of their own life in their hearts. Gale is Dead. In this society, what does that mean?

In a very real sense, Beechholme and the London school I attended, Alvering Secondary in Wandsworth, were my Centres of Racial Studies. One reinforced the other in countless ways. In Beechholme I was treated as separate and unequal: at Alvering I found out why. I came to realize that inequality was the capital of black Britain. And Britain, from my experience, in every sense was always graded into and partitioned by class and colour, red and blue, black and white.

Frequently, I lay awake at night dreading the thought of the next day's persecutions. I had reached a sensitive point, and other people's switch-offs carved up my soul. It hurt.

Contempt for my colour took many forms, from comparisons with apes to the white preoccupation with the size of the black male organ. The incredible sexual stamina blacks were supposed to possess produced the retort 'go and fuck your own kind' whenever I spoke to a white girl. Accordingly, all blacks were dirty, ignorant and stupid, they caused trouble, lived on Social Security benefits and ate smelly food. But, and this was real praise, blacks were great singers, great athletes and good in bed. Whites, on the other hand, were scientifically minded and tough, good humoured and sportsmanlike. And they had an Empire to prove it.

The social brainwashing had its desired effect. If I wanted to be better, to be like them, I had to be white. So I tried. At Easter 1960, when I was fourteen – Easter, because that was when Jesus was in the mood to forgive *all* sins and by now black had become a sin – I went down on my knees and prayed, real hard. Every time I was alone I prayed, sometimes for hours. I prayed with tears in my eyes, imploring God to listen to my plea. I prayed to God to make me white. The myth of black inferiority, having been preached at me for so long, convinced me that the way out was to become a white man.

I closed my mind to Africa, by not reading, thinking or talking about her. Whenever Africa or black people were derided I joined in the derision, albeit carefully just in case they turned on me. Moreover, whenever the topic of African or West Indian Independence hit the headlines I slunk into the background. Britain's media traditionally commented negatively on these events with 'how will they manage to look after themselves without us?', thus exposing me to further ridicule. At those moments I kept quiet while seething inside. In keeping a low profile I denied everything, myself as well.

A series of battles, throbbing my psychology, aided my denials; it was a habit. One of these was triumphant in its execution. It happened on a train journey back to Beechholme from school. As the train pulled into Belmont Station (Banstead was the next stop) I peeked out of the window and waited until the porter drew level with my compartment. I then let out a terrible groan. The porter reacted, believed what he saw and called for an ambulance. At the local hospital constipation was diagnosed. Since I intended to stay there a while, I improved very slowly. On returning to Beechholme two weeks later the pressure of racism was, for a while, much reduced.

I was still recovering eight weeks later when the unexpected happened. It was May 1960. My father, whom I had not seen since August 1953, was coming to see me, with my uncle, a member of the Royal College of Surgeons. I had mixed emotions, for what could I say when the situation I had long ceased to dream about was with me now? I saw the pain of failure written across my father's face as tears welled up in his eyes. His African dream and ambitions had ended up here in Beechholme, a children's home. I perceived the effort my father made to render harmless the abyss of time since we last met. We had a pleasant afternoon together, my father, my uncle and myself.

For many years I had lived under the head-knocking hang-up that Britain was my permanent pawnbroker. I owed. As a debtor I thought I should be grateful. But for what? What did I owe? I was tormented. I had lost my culture, I had lost my longing to see others like me. I had seen through the empty faceless smiles of those who derided me. I had so many feelings and ideas waiting to be freed. But it was impossible. As a black, white society had solitarily confined me in the middle of a crowd. Every crowd.

But something inside me stirred and stirred again, I thought back to a time when there were no rules, no aggression, no fear in the gut, just me and my beach and the wind. And I shared them with my white friend, Jonathan.

But I was psychologically violated and I began to smoulder. My pain turned to energy, fuelling my resistance. I began to rebel. I refused all help because it had been proven shallow. I spent hours with myself eating thoughts. I took advantage of everything, every ounce of knowledge, about where I was from, who *my* people were and where I was, now.

Apart from my friend, there was no warmth in this atmosphere, and I started to read and looking up from my readings, I skipped anger and went straight into rage.

Before 1962, Britain's blacks existed insensibly in a cloud of tolerance. Because of the availability of white gospel worshippers, carefully sustained by subversive white liberals, we developed no political philosophy. Ideas of 'revolution' were just the preserve of individuals. Any anglophobic bitter-mouths were coupled to black stocks on the white side of the street. Cash, making no enemies, induced some whites to cut a path for the black sellout, a 180 degree black. This shackled achiever broke out to all and sundry his confessions of 'Don't rock the boat'. Sadness melts. He came on real strong, with white handcuffs on and presented whites with the message 'I'm yours'. Due to his 'Marster', who saw him as a pile of bricks, Joe Sad lived a Christian path. It was a belly habit. He was a cupboard, a desk, a piano, a chair, in fact anything the white wanted him to be. Joe Sad walked straight into a flash pad, and stood beside the chair. Today, he is the filing cabinet, selling out verbal rip-offs. It has taken an explosion of world-wide categorical black imperatives, proclamations of black power and hosannahs of negritude to undermine this position. In time the Uncle Tom will no longer be trusted in Britain, as in America.

Nineteen sixty-two was the year that captured the essence of imperial miscalculations. It was an auspicious moment for Britain's whites who were about to reinforce their superiority. Their mood refuted those expedient colonial mythomanic promises of 'entry and Britishness'. White affections were effectively reversed, spawning the Commonwealth Immigrants Act.

It was a splendidly unguarded hour for the black and Asian newcomers who believed the promises of the 'mother country'. But the West Indians were also distracted by the West Indies Act, passed the same day as the Commonwealth Immigrants Act, promising independence from Britain. Ironically, black power at that time was not even a dream. From the moment those Acts were passed the atmosphere in this white-house changed.

The Commonwealth Immigrants Act had blown the guts out of the 'mother country' hallucination, in which blacks and Asians had been romanticizing, thumping the idea into guesswork that the black position here was very arbitrary. The Act concurred, by rendering unthinkable the psychic idea of peaceful black, brown, and white rapport in the near future.

That year left in its acrimonious wake a dismayed black and Asian presence and a racially boastful white population. The Act was seen by many whites as having put the coloureds in their place and, as if to underline this, numerous clubs all over Britain were closed to blacks overnight. Two near Wolverhampton had their own methods: Smethwick's Labour Club boasted a colour bar; Sandwell Youth Club Committee openly issued their racial bias, 'no coloured person shall be admitted to membership of the club'.

The press went to town with headlines: 'Spittoons wanted', for spitting blacks; 'More immigrants from West Indies' and 'Concern at total of Immigrants', accelerated media scoops about black and Asian immigrants and their right to be in Britain; 'Coloured folk dominating house buying' exclaimed the *Smethwick Telephone*, a West Bromwich newspaper. Conservative councillor, Norman Phillips, appealed for a 'home security trust fund', claiming that young couples were leaving Smethwick because of 'immigrant domination' in house buying. Another Conservative councillor, Donald Finney, blamed Smethwick's traditional centre of vice, Spon Lane, on 'coloured men'. He said his own wife had been accosted and white girls were associating with coloured men.

Educationalists played their part. In 1962, Terence Casey, Headmaster of St Joseph's Catholic School, Maida Vale, went even further. With a gibe at black people he denounced the Twist: 'While the people of Africa struggle to free themselves from the dark shadow of a primitive past . . . our young folk are initiated into the barbaric contortions of the Twist.'

This racial extremism touched a nerve in my system, that the framework of British society was built on a wind of sudden changes. In Britain, a nation of versatile chaos, the negative motivation of suppressing blacks in her former colonies developed into a counter-attraction, nigger culling.

Deportation became the focal talking point of the Immigration Act. In April 1962, a frosty *Daily Mail* headline announced: 'Britain to begin deporting criminals next month', suggesting that it was an unprecedented step to kick out lawbreakers not born here. In the same month some Midlands conservatives capped the *Daily Mail.* They asked the Home Secretary to 'deport immigrants who did no work within a reasonable time'. The action of racial discrimination was no longer confined to antiquated white expatriates, yesterday's Governor-Generals and District Commissioners. Now a government decree, hypnotic to negrophobic whites irrespective of class and rank, welcomed them to tread on the blacks and Asians. Complaints underlining black inferiority sprouted. Hatred was taken further and in 1963, among many repulsive incidents, came an event which startled me: Janta Singh, an Indian in Birmingham, had his grocery store bombed. The bombers had carefully packed a fire-extinguisher with explosives and planted it in the doorway of his shop.

This, I thought, was the writing on the wall for Afro-Caribasian peoples. I was hurt when I saw white friends I had known all my life ooze into obscurity and side-step the census when faced with the blemishing topic of race. From out front, white people I knew focused and measured and occupied the conscious part of my subconscious. At this time, I viewed Britain through the polemics of my school history lessons and reviewed the attitudes of her whites. I saw a people flipping out, directionless from the trickeries, triumphs and romantic legends of their history, still percolating from Empire with a racism created by myths, sustained by conquest, cemented by long-term domination and conducted with an aggressive technology. The Empire mentality was alive and well and thriving in Britain. It was not an overstatement to say that the heart of the matter is that the majority of Britain's whites don't like blacks and Asians and are having a hard time keeping it a secret. More significantly, blacks and Asians were faced with a dilemma: to be here 'gratefully' or to retaliate against the blitz-krieging media and public racism. For Britain's whites hold a cutting finesse in their arguments, of black race-reducing views repeated endlessly; coupled with a monstrous condescension which screams, 'Accept what we say. We're right, we're white'. The garage-mechanics are here. The black man has long since been the earthbound vehicle, but the white man holds the heavenly tools of supremacy.

The turbulence inside white Britain's black-panic resolved my decision. I set a new course. Iced by white hypocrisy, I confessed with a group in a house in Lavender Hill, Battersea. We listened and watched as they decided our lives and what we should do and what was going to happen to us. We listened to them crackling about us having a place in Britain. As I walked the streets, I noticed the white answers looking at me. It was then I began to realize that the depth of condescension for my colour in Britain was deeper than I wanted to believe. I came to terms with the blatant fact that racism was (and still is) latent in Britain's adult white population.

I also came to terms with another fact. I was fed up with being manoeuvred and impressionistically framed into unimportance by whites. Their belief in black subhumanity, as far as we were concerned, was so far gone that it was instinctive. They did not know how to change their own myths about us.

Decolonization, which I had once thought would give them a new picture, merely focused their attentions on how black countries would fail as independents. With the colonial departure the useless title 'Third World' was added, rubbing in second-classness and conjuring up another physical but directionless globe like a naughty moon in the paranoid white imagination.

Immigration of blacks into Britain made no room for the white mental shock experienced when they realized that those so-called 'coloureds' intended to compete. They had been enticed to assume their traditional places labouring away at jobs whites didn't want. Hence any failing black pupil gave more credibility to the white myth of black intellectual inferiority. Any black who achieved unsettled them more, having solidly identified intelligence with white.

It was up to the black to prove his intellectual capability and equality to the white who permanently 'failed' to see black achievement and was constantly deaf when he heard any black ideas. But the race competition of equalizing imperatives was on. Because of the racist attitudes of most of our teachers who taught us, with a look of 'failures' in their eyes, we helped them succeed, by failing. Realistically we knew it made little difference either way. The result, we thought by our collective experiences, was already decided. That blacks were basically factory-fodder in this nation of 'opportunities' did not encourage us to make the scene of stardom; we gave up. In other words we purposely failed, thus failing them. Anyone who succeeded was a sellout.

I began making changes as the race question distracted my attention from the lore of knowledge to the lore of the street. Street sense became a permanent picnic; I feasted with the intent of thoroughly understanding white behaviour. I got a degree in black aggression. I also became ignorant and sensitive about it; piling bricks on the head of any white who picked up on it. 'He has a chip on his shoulder.' I most certainly did, along with my white school mates. Do as you would be done by, but do it first, guided my ethics. I burned British history books and relegated their entire contents to mere lies and wishful thinking on the part of the whites. In geography, the Russian steppes could have been halfway down the Bethnal Green Road for all I cared. 1066 and all that I dismissed as pure fairytale and the white version of the slave trade was a hype and a hustle. In my destructive attitude to Britain, I hacked the whiteness out of my mind. I religiously hammered any white who tried to lay a pretentious superior intellect on my soul. This showcase nigger cased up the white show. It was quality time. When I was a negro I had many white friends, but now that I am black I have few.

I carried on running heavy black changes, I was cold. And then in October 1963 a tragedy occurred, which iced up my innards. It happened in South Africa, where the oppression of black people by whites is also a way of life.

Nelson Mandela, a former member of the African National Congress, was to be tried for sabotage and a conspiracy to overthrow a regime. Not so long before that, on 21 March 1960, during a demonstration in Sharpeville, the police opened fire on demonstrators killing sixty-nine blacks and wounding 300, while continuing to brutalize the rest. The only difference I could see between Sharpeville and Mandela's crisis was that it was occasionally necessary for white South Africa to demonstrate to the world her nodding acquaintance with her own one-sided statute laws in relation to blacks. It struck me that in a land where whites *devised* the constitution, by sowing racism into it and thus into the law, all blacks stood a sure chance of being guilty of everything. In a country where racial vindictiveness explodes the lives of black people with such immoral amorality, Mandela and others were convicted and sentenced long before they came to trial. However, our group, pained by that injustice, defended Mandela and anyone who used violence in similar situations.

I screamed with fury, not only at Mandela's prosecution, but also at the attitude adopted by Britain's whites towards his dilemma. Was he or was he not guilty, seemed to be the basis of their questioning, never seriously challenging the life-blood of such a brutal regime. But at the same time, with shallow profundity, they carefully examined the ability of black Africans to govern their own countries after Independence. Intuitively I felt that their demeanour could only be so because of the psychogenic similarities of the Africaaners and Britain's whites. It dawned on me that their only dissimilarities lay in method and sophistication.

In comparison to South Africa and America, British race relations are apparently harmonious. But the truth of the matter is that these so-called relations are an edifice, a cardboard façade and rotten to the core. In reality the British are more subtle than the South Africans, being older at the game, and do not need 'Whites Only' signs with which to do their discriminating. But the result is similar in its effect. South Africa's racism enforces the oppression of black people by Statute Law and legislates against all forms of demonstration by blacks fighting against the very laws forbidding them to demonstrate.

In fact Britain's whites out-Herod Herod, with Machiavellian determination, evaluating blacks and Asians with the stake they hold in the racism of the doctrine of white sovereignty. Not unlike the South Africans, but with their own highly refined version of *apartheid,* tried and tested with whole-hogging success on Britain's working classes and women, the whites now practise with subtlety a sophisticated form of subjugation on Britain's blacks and Asians.

But Britain's blithe spirit, grounded in racial condescension, is being demolished brick by brick. With black equality, of every kind, slapping him in the face, his new question is '*If this savage is as talented as myself, then what have I been all along?*' In Britain, the black, white racial equality yardstick is under hypercritical invasion and is being burned in a wind of searing black heat. The product of an ex-slave's memory.

In all my years here, I have always lived with some apprehension. I, like some other blacks and Asians, function and act with an over-the-horizon psychology covering both shoulders. The black man's thoughts of reactive aggression have always been decided by white race prejudice. The relationship between black and white is a savage reality, the naked result of which can be seen in South Africa. For pain exists in every heart, irrespective of colour, which believes in what should be the first principles of mankind – humanity and human rights. If the black man living in Britain reacts, it will be akin to a razor-blade slicing through white thoughts. The pain is great.

I have some white friends, those friends principally being people who genuinely accept me as I am and consider my views as valid as their own. I have grown close to them and skin colour is not a subject worth any consideration, everything else is. Outside this circle fear is intuitive, which teaches me that it is necessary to

15

retain a traditional black opaque indefinable distance from those whites I don't know.

But I still have hope, because I am an aggressive worshipper of optimism. I don't know any other way. I have hope in the youth of Britain, black and white. A youth who recognize their interdependence, unlike their parents. For this nation badly needs imaginations to be stimulated for its survival. There is hope, too, in its few but much-travelled wide-eyed citizens who cannot go along in its crazy flirtation with disaster. They refuse to believe in the governing ethic which has been using yesterday's ideas. Tradition stabilizes Britain and holds it back at the same time. The Britannic Dilemma.

Nevertheless, many white youths cannot see how they can be schooled often intimately with black youth and then on reaching adulthood be asked to tread on the friendships of their past. They cannot believe in the directionless course of Britain's declining power; in preterite myths of superiority and contemporary political reactionaries, left or right.

I was shocked into race reality, at a time when labelling anyone 'coloured' denoted inferiority. A time when Britain's black and Asian population accepted second best with little or no complaint. But as we enter a new epoch, black youth here will no longer accept the subordination meted out to their parents. They are saying, 'we have something to contribute' and 'gimme, it's our right'. The 'right' is theirs, and surely they will take it. Their struggle may transmit no organization recognizable from outside, but it will make sense. If whites wish to know where to start with blacks and Asians, the answer is to stop. Stop patronizing, stop harassing and stop treating them as educationally sub-normal. Stop assuming that if a black is not an Uncle Tom, then he has a chip on his shoulder.

Stories discovered afterwards have always far more depth than the rumours circulated before. But before those stories can be related, the individual's curiosity is paramount. For understanding to be reached, that curiosity has to be satisfied. Curiosity is the essence. The essence I speak of here is black and Asian. Only now is there a story to relate. Tell on, tell all, tell everything.

2
Rule Britannia

Great Britain is a land of class, where the national perception is white. Numerous realities dictate the way each class makes the life of black and Asian people *in general* more awkward. But the contemporary race quarrel of black versus white is making certain that British internal exploration, with determination, has begun.

When Britain abolished her part in the slave trade in 1833, black people regained their 'freedom', although they had been in Britain since the early part of the sixteenth century, when the white man's definition of freedom for blacks was created, which has changed only in degrees to this day. The guilt of morals is the space between fact and fiction. The fundamentals of British racism are hidden in the music of yesterday's Empire builders, in slavery. In 1562, the first British slave undertaker, John Hawkins, was backed by Queen Elizabeth I, who gave him a ship, ironically named the *Jesus*, with which he pursued a commission of slavery which became perpetually beneficial to the British nation. Hard on the heels of Hawkins's Honourable Company of Merchant Adventurers was a band of myth-makers – churchmen, traders and racial scientists – which was eager to evolve justifiable reasons for British greed.

Slave merchants returning with slaves and an avalanche of

myths found a tonic in the theories of those skin-beating evolution scientists and clergy who liberally sprinkled 'biology' with 'Christian morals' and 'God's will', as a guilt-relieving agent. The black race was therefore justified into eternal slavery.

But the cry of the slave remains, so the clocks must be turned back and the act of slavery must be reviewed so that it can evoke a flash-back in order to comprehend the magnitude of the black man's stake in white Britain.

The immoralities and inhumanities which froze the souls of millions of slaves can only begin to assume their proper place in the British economic memory, if it is recognized that this is a land where the profit motive cuts down everything in its path. Which explains why John Hawkins was knighted by Queen Elizabeth for his success 'to take the inhabitants with burning and spoiling their towns'. You may think this an understandable attitude towards other peoples in the context of the rampant violence of Elizabethan England. But what we shall perceive is that Britain's savage treatment of black slaves was malignant; that there exists an active affinity between the treatment of black people as slaves, their treatment in Britain's colonies under the Pax Britannica, and the treatment black people are receiving in Britain today.

The history of oppression of black peoples by whites is two-fold. The first is the slave trade, which was followed by the second, a ruthless military fractionalization which was covered up by a coating of mendacity called the Pax Britannica, to become the British Empire. It is the first that we must turn our attention to.

Through the first slave, white men created their sum total of a black man, at the same time affirming that for their creation the white fantasy of heaven would be the black's hell, on earth. When the first African was kidnapped by Britannic whites and thrown into the hold of a ship by some bovine ruffian to become a slave, he anchored white ideas of his earthbound hell. And the apparent willingness of the slaves to offer themselves, not in a trickle but a torrent of millions, gave even more foundation to the white myth of their sub-humanity. Failure to outwit their slave-masters was seen by those whites as justification for black enslavement.

Slavery was not only 'Made in Britain'; the hands of every European power are also smeared with black blood. Their gruesome 'family business' became a multi-national enterprise when Columbus 'discovered' America.

When Spain struck gold in Hispaniola, now Haiti, white enslavement of black people became imperative and the infamous Middle Passage to the New World was activated. Spain in the sixteenth century contracted with Portugal who was to supply Spain with a steady supply of black slaves for her West Indian and American colonies. The Dutch won that right from Portugal in 1685, and kept it until 1702, when France grabbed it and kept it until 1713.

Under an arrangement of special contracts aptly named the 'Asiento de Negros', Spain conferred on any individual, company or nation the exclusive right to supply black slaves for its American colonies. Sir John Hawkins was one such individual, but Britain won this coveted glittering prize in 1713, under the Treaty of Utrecht, making her the 'greatest slave trader in the world'. She obtained an 'absolute monopoly of the supply of slaves to the Spanish Colonies'. This was at that time considered to be a 'sound piece of mercantile policy'. The monopoly was in turn given to the South Sea Company by the British government.

The British take pride in their sophisticated accumulation of historical documents. Yet historical records, pertaining to blacks, have been loosely retained or filed away as unwanted memories – the only records of blacks kept faithfully by whites are their criminal records. How many slaves the British transported, for example, from Africa to make a profit for themselves in the West Indies and the Americas, has been quoted in British history books as ranging from one million to ten million landed alive. It is ironic that a country boastful of its business and accountancy methods can only approximate to within a few million the number of slaves it actually exported. The records of the Port of Liverpool, for instance, are remarkably explicit. Between 1783 and 1793, 921 ships from that port carried 303,737 slaves who landed alive, to the total value of £15,186,850. According to the Economics Division of the Bank of England, at 1981 prices this sum is now £350 million.

In Britain, when everything else fails, they call out the record books of white fears about black numbers in Britain, black crime, black failure, black inability and white intellectual predominance. By this method, they can fetter a moment of turmoil which undermines the black and brown community. Other whites can, with underhand dealings, strategically manoeuvre black people along with their own devious interests. The result of the 1970 general election, an election laced with immigration as its main issue, is an example of this malignant technique.

It is no accident that I chose the election of 1970 to comment upon. In 1968, through Britain's Moses, Enoch Powell, race took on a new status becoming a problem with clear grit. 'Rivers of blood' was the subject chosen by a man with no political power other than his overriding ambition. As an indefatigable slithering adder his immigration sums had great scare-power, swallowing up the Church-like pretence of many phoney liberal attitudes. And the fight against any black revolution was on.

Moreover, in the highly structured class hierarchy which forms British society, the blacks lie on the bottom. People at the bottom of any society have little control over the transmitted information, or lack of information, put out or not put out by others about themselves. It follows and is perfectly logical that anything and everything can and is written about black people without any possibility of redress.

When blacks were first enslaved by the British in the racial dimsightedness of that period, it was thought that they should be slaves because they convinced themselves they possessed no souls. A rational argument. It was also a rational argument that Ian Smith's illegal Unilateral Declaration of Independence in 1965 would find fertile ground among his kith and kin over here in Britain. The Achilles' heel of Britain's justifying arguments for not sending troops to end the oppression of Zimbabwean blacks by their mercenary white Rhodesian kin-folk was, 'they fought beside us during the Second World War', showing us the quick-change artistry of British morality.

What Britons conveniently forgot was that blacks from their Empire fought beside them in a variety of places including the march on Jerusalem and Damascus with General Allenby during the First World War. In addition they fought at Gallipoli and Mesopotamia. The Indians went further, raising for Britain's beloved Empire the largest volunteer army in history. A mere one and a half million men. What my own father, attached to the West African Frontier Force, was doing fighting the Japanese in Burma has never been clear, the Japanese having never perpetrated any act of violence against blacks.

British morality is clear cut and has always been. In the slave trade they said, 'toil for us' and millions of slaves did and died in huge quantities. In the colonies, during their wars against each other, they said 'fight for us' and hundreds of thousands of blacks and Asians did and died for their trouble. Today the attitude still is, as it has always been, 'what ever good you do, we'll never recognize it and what's more we'll always forget it'.

According to Britain's two-tiered definition of morality in the nineteenth century, black people were menials and heathens. Therefore, ill-treatment of black people at the hands of whites was seen as their rightful lot. That was British custom and the popular feeling at that time. Time merely changed their methods and their morality towards blacks imprinting itself into the Briton's psychogenesis prevented them from recognizing that making black profit through colonization was an equally oppressive subtle form of slavery.

In twentieth-century Britain little has changed. Many black and Asian people have died and have been brutalized in outrageous circumstances, some in police stations, others on the streets. There are those who have been terrorized and discriminated against without any form of redress. All these acts in the eyes of whites merely warrant a cursory investigation, the result of which is always a foregone conclusion. But the death of white school teacher Blair Peach, in 1979, sent a shock-wave of revulsion throughout Britain and one inquiry was not enough. The inference was obvious. White morality is clear cut but Blair Peach, because he was on the side of the blacks, still lost out. On hearing that an act of social or physical brutality has been committed against Britain's blacks or Asians, Britain's whites take a moral holiday.

Inside the racial arrogance of the British exists a crooked device known as *historical chauvinism*, through which can be seen the most spectacular attempt in human history by indifference, non-acknowledgement and conscienceless white injustice, the attempted erasure of black history since the beginning of Britain's trade in slaves. And blacks and to a lesser extent Asians, controlled by whites since that slave period, having no control over the records of slavery and white colonial administrations, have phenomenal difficulty in preventing that attempted erasure. The *West Indian World*, a black community newspaper, recognizing that black youths are not taught about their past, prints regular columns on black history.

If Britain's blacks and Asians want somewhere to attack, they should attack the archives of the British government and make them print whatever records are still in existence about their shameful trade in slaves, print everything about the valuable black and Asian contribution toward their two great wars in which they involved almost everyone else, and print their records of economic trickery and physical violence committed on black and Asian peoples in their ex-colonies. It is all history now, and history is something we should learn from, not live in.

But we must look again at the wartime contribution of black and Asian peoples in chapter three in order that an important part of a people's history be categorized into its proper place.

It is remarkable that the popular slave trade story of how the blacks sold each other, a get-out clause, persisted for so many years; and how the mainstream of Britain's whites have expediently remained in ignorance in their perceptions of black people and their myths about blacks. The recipe for how this fraud was worked and how it was used necessitates inquiry at this stage.

It is important to quote E.D. Morel, a British Reformist, who *The Times* credited as 'the most important factor in awakening both public and official opinion to the monstrous iniquity . . . perpetrated with ever-increasing cynicism and effrontery in the Congo Basin.' His book, *The Black Man's Burden*, published in 1920, contains a description of the vicious methods used by British slave-catchers:

> The trade had grown so large that mere kidnapping raids conducted by white men in the immediate neighbourhood of

the coast-line were quite insufficient to meet its requirements. Regions inaccessible to the European had to be tapped by the *organisation* of civil wars. The whole of the immense region from the Senegal to the Congo, and even further south, became in the course of years convulsed by incessant internecine struggles. A vast tumult reigned from one extremity to the other of the most populous and fertile portions of the continent. Tribe was bribed to fight tribe, community to raid community. To every native chief, as to every one of his subjects, was held out the prospect of gain at the expense of his neighbour. Tribal feuds and individual hatreds were alike intensified, and while wide stretches of countryside were systematically ravaged by organised bands of raiders armed with muskets, 'hunting down victims for the English trader whose blasting influence, like some malignant providence extended over mighty regions where the face of a white man was never seen.'

. . . Queen Anne saw no objection, it is said, to increase her dowry, like her celebrated predecessor, from its operations. A statute of King William of pious memory affirms that 'the trade was highly beneficial to the kingdom'; another of George II declared it to be 'very advantageous to Great Britain,' and 'necessary to the plantations,' while the 'Society for propagating Christianity,' including half the episcopal bench, derived, as masters, from the labour of their slaves in the West Indies, an income which they spent in 'teaching the religion of peace and goodwill to men.' [My italics]

But the ever-victorious British were still not converted to the idea that it was unworkable to exist as dependants on the backs of their black victims. With an interest in guaranteeing white working-class approval for a political list of immoral doings, Britain's ruling and trading elite with resourceful vision fabricated yet another myth. The Empire, it was said, only possessed immense tracts of land in Africa because those lands were wasting away. And those black inhabitants were wickedly lazy. In that continent, as in Britain at one time, the heart of the matter lay in the land.

With the experience gained from depriving Britain's working classes of land, the ruling and trading classes went into action once more. The formula was, separate the blacks from their land thus transforming them into titleless wage earners and their dependence on their new bosses would be assured.

The truth of the matter was, and still is in minority white-ruled South Africa, that a foreign body had dispossessed black people of their land, demolished their way of life and assaulted the bedrock of their freedom. On reflection, and in the searchlight of contemporary racial reality, the infliction of such bondage can only be preserved by the unwavering use of violence.

The difference between Britain's working classes and African peoples since colonization is that Britain's have-nots' attentions are being diverted by sophisticated consumer items and public facilities that soften life.

Conversely, then as now, Africa's masses without the distractions acquired by Britain's working classes, without a profusion of choices, depend almost completely on the land and its uses. Britain had perceived in her slaves a way of developing, not Africa, but her interests in the Americas and the West Indies. In the racial myopia of the nineteenth century, she looked hungrily again at Africa, revised her original conception of her interest in that continent and 'discovered' an enormous deposit of manpower and a gigantic store of untapped material resources, fundamental to her new-fashioned industry. The temptation to impress that man-power force into her employ, this time in Africa itself, proved too powerful. Colonization had finally arrived and with it the policy, first devised when trading in slaves, of setting 'tribe against tribe and community against community'. 'Divide and rule' was once again put into action.

An example of the methods used, gleaned from Britain's experience in the slave trade, was the story of Rhodesia, now known as Zimbabwe. Albert Henry George Grey who later became Earl Grey, Governor-General of Canada, wrote:

> Throughout this part of the British Dominions the coloured people are generally looked upon by the whites as an inferior race, whose interest ought to be systematically disregarded when they come into competition with their own, and who ought to be governed mainly with a view to the advantage of the

superior race. And for this advantage two things are considered to be specially necessary: First, that facilities should be afforded to the White colonists for obtaining possession of land heretofore occupied by the native tribes; and secondly, that the Kaffir population should be made to furnish as large and as cheap a supply of labour as possible. [Quoted in E.D. Morel's *The Black Man's Burden*]

This razored summary of colonial attitudes reveals the stance taken by Britain's whites towards the peoples within their African, West Indian and Asian colonies. In October 1888, the following epic occurred:

Chief Lobengula, of the then ruling race, the Amandebele, was approached by Cecil Rhodes and his conspiring companion Charles Rudd. They were in pursuit of concessions 'for a place to dig for gold'. Their idea of 'a place' became encapsulated in a document signed between themselves and Chief Lobengula. It was the blue-print for Britain's acquisitive mentality abroad, euphemistically known as exploration. Under its terms, in exchange for a monthly payment of £100 and British products in the shape of 1,000 Martini-Henry rifles and 100,000 rounds of ball cartridges, Rhodes and Rudd were to receive 'the complete and exclusive charge over all the metals and minerals' in Zimbabwe, together with 'full power to do all things that they may deem necessary to win and procure the same, and to hold, collect and enjoy the profits and revenues, if any derivable from the said metals and minerals'.

This multi-purpose exploitative document, known as the Rhodes-Rudd Concession, eventually became the basis for the initial British occupation of Zimbabwe, and finally the foundation of the white Rhodesian self-styled Constitution.

At that time few whites realized or cared how many blacks would have to die in order to regain what was rightfully theirs, and what had been deceitfully gotten by the exploring hands of white Rhodesians, Britain's sons. As far as they were concerned a black-dominated Zimbabwe under a black Prime Minister, as Rhodesia's wonderman Ian Smith himself believed, was a 'thousand years away'.

While white Rhodesians turned the original black landowners into subjects without security, they also began to do everything in their power to goad the Amandebele and the Mashonas into rebellion. This they did by setting up courts, and the British South Africa Company which was not a sovereign power, but had gained Britain's imperial assent, also carried out executions.

Under Leander Starr Jameson, BSAC's manager in Africa and incidentally the instigator of the Jameson raid into Transvaal, the Company's divisive plans came to fruition in July 1893. They began by stealing cattle from the Mashonas which they had hired from Lobengula, chief of the Amandebele. Jameson informed Lobengula that the cattle theft had been carried out by the Mashonas who had no intention of returning his cattle. Cattle being a sovereign symbol, the theft of which is an affront to the entire tribe, Lobengula punished the Mashonas in an avenging expedition in which several Mashonas were killed. Captain Lendy, under the direct orders of Jameson, completed the Company's plans by shooting thirty Amandebele warriors dead as they were retreating from their confrontation with the Mashonas. Jameson pleaded self-defence: no white lost his life.

The 'divide' completed, the climate was right for their 'rule' to be put into effect. Lobengula was invaded by the British South Africa Company, with the British government mouthing protests but doing nothing, setting the precedent for its procrastinating attitude seventy-two years later, when Ian Smith declared Rhodesia's UDI in 1965. The British South Africa Company's Loot Committee appropriated 6,000 square miles of land and slavery, through forced labour, returned. Lobengula died in January 1894.

In a letter to King George V, quoted in E.D. Morel's *The Black Man's Burden,* members of Lobengula's family wrote:

> The members of the late King's [Lobengula's] family, your petitioners, and several members of the tribe are now scattered about on farms so parcelled out to white settlers, and are practically created a nomadic people living in this scattered condition, under a veiled form of slavery, they being not allowed individually to cross from one farm to another, or from

place to place except under a system of permit or pass and are practically forced to do labour on these private farms as a condition of their occupying land in Matabeleland.

Who created apartheid?
In his book, *The Heart of Africa*, published in 1954, Alexander Campbell quoted a friend who delivered a penetrating truism:

The black man in a white dominated society, said Hans Leuenberger, is equipped with X-ray eyes. He not only can study and understand the white man's techniques, but can see inside the white man's mind, penetrate his thoughts, and follow his motivations. But the white man only sees black bodies. He has never entered into the black man's thoughts, does not know what is going on in his heart, and seldom speaks his language.

That home truth fuses Britain's past with her present.
Brutality and injustice towards black and brown peoples as a British way of life did not end in Africa. Suppressive methods tried and tested during Britain's trade selling black human beings, crowned with success, promoted the use of the same racist formula in her colonies.

In Britain's international career of racial gangsterism and banditry, the West Indians, too, felt the long arm of her oppression. These blacks were divided through the slave trade and ruled by sheer terror from the moment they landed on those faraway islands where a selection of Britain's landed gentry as plantation owners, busily building the financial base of their twentieth-century fortunes and estates, unleashed their pitiless inhumanities on defenceless blacks.

On 11 October 1856, in Jamaica, a crowd of blacks went to Morant Bay court-house to complain about the heavy-handed treatment meted out to blacks found squatting on uncultivated land. In reply to this protest, the white authorities murdered seven of the so-called rioters, who in turn killed two hated white overseers. In the words of James Morris, writing in *Pax Britannica*, the then Governor of Jamaica, Edward John Eyre, characteristically put down the demonstration: 'with unusually ferocious zeal, killing or executing more than six hundred people, flogging six hundred more, and burning down a thousand homes . . .'

Quoting from *Colour, Class and the Victorians* by Professor Douglas A. Lorimer, the press reaction was:

> On 4 November *The Times* declared that this latest news from Jamaica proved that blacks were unsuited to freedom.
>
> On 11 November the *Standard* admitted that little news had been received of the insurrection, surveyed previous slave revolts in Jamaica, and concluded that black rebellions were far worse than white ones. The indolent black savages of Jamaica, the *Standard* claimed, had no grievances, but sought only to satisfy their greed, hatred, and lust for white property, white lives, and white women.

The voice of the *Standard* set the formula for the master-plan on how black and brown protests and rebellions against white authority in the twentieth century should and would be treated by the British media and their readers, listeners and viewers. Do you remember the media reports concerning the unsuitability of the independencies of Britain's West Indian possessions, of India, Pakistan, Kenya, Nigeria, Tanzania, Ghana, Somalia, Zambia, and Zimbabwe, etc?

The Pax Britannica was a pretentious and self-glorious deception, maybe not in British eyes but certainly in the eyes of blacks and Asians. The black and white definitions of their 'Peace' were always totally opposed. Britain's idea of peace was a violent nightmare both to blacks whom they had brutalized and murdered over three centuries, and to Asians whom they ritually had 'blown from cannon'. In the words of James Morris in *Heaven's Command*, Indians were tied 'to the muzzles of guns and blown to pieces to the beat of drums'.

But the magnificent imperfection of the British Empire, which was also its latent strength, was distance; due to the far-flungness of its imperial territories, it was impossible for a counter-revolution to be mounted by its unenthusiastic constricted black and brown peoples, acting in concert.

Take India, the jewel in the British crown. After a century of persecution, in 1857, the Indians fought against the British Raj, which slid into British history as the Indian Mutiny. We are told that the misnamed Mutiny was the result of Indian resentment at Britain's issue of animal-fat greased cartridges, which were offensive to Hindu and Muslim soldiers. That was the advertised fantasy. In reality, the rebellion was due to enforced Christianization and also the fact (expediently dismissed by Britain's history books) that India's masses hated the British presence in their country and had always done so.

In the sheer desperation of the British to remain on what was seen as priceless territory, they were unable to recognize in the determination of the so-called mutineers in the act of their rebellion, a conqueror's maxim. 'In Imperialism', wrote William Inge, in his *Outspoken Essays in Patriotism*, 'nothing fails like success.' What has gone down in Britain's books as a 'mutiny' must at the very least be re-recorded as India's First War of Independence.

However, while the British Raj jackbooted its mark into the heart of India, but not the Indians, it was never a secret to the majority of trigger-happy British individuals there, that India's masses resented the colonial administration and were always psychologically in rebellion against them. They succeeded in subverting Indian resentment and agitation in 1857. But to ensure that the crown-jewel remained in Britain's keeping, a tighter round-the-clock watch was kept. Through a system of paid Indian informers, India's powerful Princes and the Indian Civil Service, (ICS), the divide and the rule was maintained with spasmodic bursts of military repression.

Furthermore, it was the Princes, some of whom were rulers of states geographically larger than Britain, who were India's sell-outs, her Uncle Toms. Thomas Macaulay, a member of the East India Company's Supreme Council, put British social engineering in the following context. If Britain was to succeed in India she had: 'to form a class of interpreters between us and the natives we govern, a class of persons Indian in blood and colour but English in tastes, in opinions, in morals and in intellect'. The Princes and darker-skinned individuals joining the Indian Civil Service aptly fitted this description: 'Moulded by nannies, tutors, advisers, the example of visiting officials and perhaps the schooling of Eton and Oxford, many of the princes became quasi-Englishmen themselves – English aristocrats buffed to an oriental polish.' (James Morris, *Pax Britannica*)

In other words, they were glorified house-boys and could be trusted to hold for Britain's whites what was not theirs in the first place. But in 1947, under the pressure of increasing violence, Britain pulled out of her 250-year Indian freehold in seventy-three days as 200,000 Indians died. The drama on the Indian sub-continent was over.

But we must look again at the slave trade in order to examine the role of the Abolitionists.

It is true that William Wilberforce, Thomas Clarkson, Granville Sharp and Secretaries of the British and Foreign Anti-Slavery Societies, John Tredgold and John Scoble, campaigned to abolish the British slave trade. But the trade was becoming an increasingly unprofitable stumbling block. And in keeping with the liberating ideal of changing one thing by replacing it with something similar, Wilberforce proposed alleviating white guilt by turning that stumbling block into stepping stones, with the perceptive introduction of Colonization, Commerce and Christianity.

Colonization, being a veiled form of slavery, was acceptable to the Abolitionists, and more than acceptable to the liberal ideal. The ideal of liberalism is the outcome of the basest instinct subscribed to by those who hold immense prejudices, but don't want to be seen obviously believing in malevolent practices, be they of a racial or class nature. But if those liberals also have something to lose in the way of status or property, that malevolence assumes another dimension.

As a result, it was necessary to manufacture for public consumption an illusion tinged with benevolent integrity, namely an Empire with Pax attached.

Ironically, those 'humane and determined men' (E.D Morel) never had any intention of radically altering the very idea of slavery. Any change they intended was purely cosmetic. In fact, the Abolitionists had every intention of reinforcing Britain's hand in the trade by submerging out of international sight the unpleasant visual aspects of it which offended delicate liberal sensibilities.

The Abolitionists' heirs, the present-day liberals, wracked with guilt by the obscene deeds of their ancestors, advertise their moral concern under a facade in which they attempt to rationalize away Britain's historical contempt for black people, by implying that Britain's slave trade was an inexplicable accident of long-gone generations, thus almost succeeding in turning the painful black reality of having been slaves into a legend.

Yesterday's abolitionists and today's liberals are one and the same. From the following accounts taken from Professor Lorimer's book, *Colour, Class and the Victorians*, can you recognize patterns and personalities?

> When painting 'The Anti-Slavery Convention', in 1840, Benjamin Haydon devised a test of abolitionist attitudes. As each noted philanthropist sat to be sketched for the painting, Haydon asked him where Henry Beckford, an ex-slave from Jamaica, should be placed in the picture. First the painter tested John Scoble and John Tredgold, Secretaries of the British and Foreign Anti-Slavery Society. Both men objected to the Negro occupying a prominent place on the same level as the leading abolitionists.

An attitude reminiscent of those whites from Oxfam, War on Want, Christian Aid, the British Council, etc.? They persistently and religiously work 'helping' develop their 'Third World', but why are there no blacks and Asians in any significant capacity on their committees? Do they forget them at the planning stages of what can only be described as their guilt-alleviating projects? Back to Professor Lorimer:

> The abolitionists' concern for the slave did not necessarily lead to an acceptance of the free Negro as a brother and equal . . . A few regarded a black skin and slave origins as a sign of inferiority, but rarely did they openly display these feelings through hostile or insulting behaviour.

Zilpha Elaw, black American preacher who toured England from 1841 to 1846, reported of her meeting with the Board of the British and Foreign Anti-Slavery Society:

> It was really an august assembly; their dignity appeared so redundant, that they scarcely knew what to do with it all. Had I attended there on a matter of life or death, I think I could scarcely have been more closely interrogated or more rigidly examined; from the reception I met with, my impression was, that they imagined I wanted some pecuniary or other help from them; for they treated me as the proud do the needy. [Quoted in Lorimer's *Colour, Class and the Victorians*]

The slave trade had been important and indispensable to the health and wealth of Britain. And the expansion of the cities of Liverpool and Bristol was due almost completely to the trade and, crucially, it kept vast numbers of those cities' labour pool employed, e.g. in shipyards, seamen and ships' chandlers, etc. Obviously, there was much to lose. As compensation to British slave merchants for the loss of their slave cargoes, the Abolitionists struck upon palm oil as a substitute. Palm oil was an ingredient necessary for the production of lubricants, candles and soap.

Hence, what Wilberforce and Co. failed, or rather avoided, to tell the British public, was that the same barbarities practised against black people in their slave trade, would again be employed in making those Africans toil for them, producing oil from the palm. And if colonization were achieved, the Abolitionists' expectations of trade in a variety of resources and minerals would be realized. In other words, the slave trade was disguised as legitimate trade.

The Abolitionists, steeped in Britain's mythical tradition of fair play and justice for all, were well aware that that tradition depended comprehensively on how it was seen, and who saw it. Therefore, whatever diabolical deeds were vented on black and brown skulls by whites, outside the white public gaze or knowledge, did not happen. And cruelties committed by whites against blacks in their colonies, firstly during their palm oil trade, and thereafter in every other trade, either, according to whites, bore little substance or did not exist. That opinionated attitude never really questioned by Britannic whites, has lived on into the twentieth century.

Naturally, to consummate their soul-saving pilgrimage, the Abolitionists proposed reforming Africa's blacks by spreading the gospel of the Christian way of life, by a down-payment for Christianity through religious imperialism. William Wilberforce wrote:

> Let us endeavour to strike *our* roots into *their* soil by the gradual introduction and establishment of *our* own principles and opinions; of *our* laws, institutions and manners; above all, as the source of every other improvement, of *our* religion, and consequently of *our* morals. [Quoted in James Morris's *Heaven's Command*. My italics.]

Through this statement can be glimpsed accurately the intentions of Wilberforce and Co. And to accomplish what should now be called the *Wilberforce Doctrine*, the racial revolutionaries stampeded into the membership of the Kingdom of God: the Church Missionary Society, Baptist Missionary Society, London Missionary Society and the British and Foreign Bible Society. This way they could with evangelical determination, teach what they saw as Africa's stone-age relics the virtues of what those 'black children' would eventually classify as an intransigent white hypocrisy, conducted in the name of Christ.

Bishop Heber also lent his religious talents with his composition, 'From Greenland's Icy Mountains', with one notable verse ending in, 'The heathen in his blindness, bows down to wood and stone'. Sentiments of betterness, but understandable considering the racial indigestion rampant in that era. But what necessitated the singing of this intolerant religious lyric in the era of Queen Elizabeth II?

However, the clergy of the Church of England along with their soul-siblings, the Roman Catholic Church, during the slave trade justified slavery and soothed their inward monitors by re-writing a certain Christian doctrine: that the righteous possessed a heavenly incentive and sinners were heading for hell (which, as we have seen, for some began on earth). Their new version of this doctrine was: since whites were morally superior to blacks, white maltreatment of blacks did not blot out any heaven credits, and thus did not bar their way to the long awaited appointment with the Right Hand of God. It should also be remembered that at this time, the clergy consisted of men who had long grown accustomed to seeing poor whites executed for petty theft and transported for petty offences. And while witnessing crimes against blacks and poor whites, their horror of injustice was tempered by the property-owning motives of the landed classes and their own.

The paramount issue on which the Churches have been consistently united is that of property and the property motive. Being slave and plantation owners themselves explains their belief in the upholding of the rules and regulations regarding the rights of property owners. Their vested property interest permitted no difference in their attitude to the commerce surrounding livestock and that of black human beings. But in accepting the concept of the abolition of slavery, the clergy implicitly accepted the concept of losing a vital and lucrative source of income. No capitalist does that.

The idea of colonization through missionary work became more determined when its financial significance was realized. Through their new religious imperialism, many more territories could be conquered and their old slavery income, with the help of their respective governments, would at the very least be quadrupled. The religious advocates set forth to conquer yesterday's slaves by moral crucifixion, resurrecting them through conversion as new loyal and ardent Jesus freaks, holding aloft the banner of Christ while through a whitewashed slavery, they filled the bottomless coffers of the Protestant and Catholic Church.

Meanwhile, having enthused their own flock with spiritual fervour, they reinforced in them a conviction that the lateness of the coming of the Messiah was due to the fact that there were so many black sinners at large. A big clean-up was needed and it must begin in Africa (what better place to begin than Africa?). The conversion-anthem rose to a crescendo, and the Church along with the Abolitionists announced a mission of good works led by Salvationists with banner headlines declaring that the well-being of

Africa's spirit-rappers was justification for their intended crusade. True to imperialistic type, it was not long before their initial aims of furthering God's work gave way to their meddling in African affairs.

It follows, with their African and Asian experience, that contemporary clergymen in Britain have transformed themselves into the 'Mouth and Ears of Black Grievances' and 'Apologists for Black Behaviour', the blacks and Asians considered to be incapable of defending or speaking for themselves.

The moral lesson is that blacks and Asians have white overseers, and conversely, those overseers have blacks and Asians. But the basis of Britain's truths is determined by the overseers and today it is no secret that those truths clash in practically every way with the life of each black and Asian individual.

The upshot being, in the everyday scenario of British life, that *truth* has come to be accepted as *customary*. Implicit in that fixed condition, it is for instance the custom to discriminate against women, and to ignore the poor and aged. It is also customary to oppress and degrade blacks and Asians and mark them as the source of Britain's problems, e.g., Britain's economic decline, unemployment, housing shortages, declining services and overpopulation requiring black and Asian immigration controls.

In a nutshell, there are those who, steeped in immorality, constantly strum trite racial remarks and speeches, and those who design Race Relations laws, head to tail with the others who congregate either silently or visibly under the National Front or British Movement banners.

3
A Savage Culture

The price of black and Asian independence in the twentieth century alone, has been very high. In a very real sense World War One was the beginning of the struggle for independence from Britain. In the words of A. J. P. Taylor in *English History 1914-1945*;

> The white populations of the Empire rallied eagerly to the mother country. Some 50 million Africans and 250 million Indians were involved, without consultation, in a war of which they understood nothing against an enemy who was also unknown to them.

With a vengeance, the Great War provided black and Asian people with the beginnings of their apprenticeship for freedom. And for some, almost immediately, poison gas proved to be that freedom's epitaph. In 1915, at Ypres, Belgium, Germany, who possessed the poison gas, was the enemy. In an account based on the first use of this terrible weapon, A J. P. Taylor as Editor-in-Chief of *The Illustrated History of the World Wars*, wrote about the German testing of this new weapon in actual battle conditions:

The area selected was a quiet four-mile stretch of front at the northern corner of the Ypres salient. The line was held by French colonial troops whose erratic tactics and discipline had been a source of friction between the British and French commanders for some weeks. Ill-fitted to resist a determined conventional attack, they collapsed immediately under the impact of this new and frightening weapon . . . Sir John French staged a series of ill-managed and extravagant counter-attacks against the new enemy positions (the British troops were told to protect themselves against gas by dipping their handkerchiefs in a solution of water and Boric acid and tying them across their mouths). These achieved little except the destruction of two brigades of the Indian Army and the dismissal of Sir Horace Smith-Dorrien, the first – and last – senior commander to protest against the cost in casualties of repetitive frontal attacks.

The 'destruction of two brigades of the Indian Army', referred to above actually meant a loss of 6,000 men who just happened to be Indian. It is also significant that the only losses suffered by Germany's enemies in that battle were blacks fighting for France and Indians dying for Britain.

Historically, with reference to black and Asian capability and the contribution to Britain, *accidental amnesia* is the guiding principle of the white British state of mind. Take Mary Seacole, a black born in Jamaica in 1805. She developed drugs which significantly reduced the loss of life in both the 1850 Kingston cholera epidemic and the 1853 yellow fever epidemic of Jamaica.

But it was her activities in the Crimean War in 1854 that have been erased from the amnesia-prone British memory. Turned down by the Crimean Fund, who refused to send her to the Crimea along with the white nurses they did send, Mary Seacole, with the assistance of a relative, paid her own fare to make the 3,000 mile journey from London to the Crimea. With her own funds she established the 'British Hospital' in the war zone. And like Florence Nightingale, whose lamp was mostly spent burnishing Britain's newspapers, Mary Seacole dispensed aid to the sick and wounded. William Russell, war correspondent for *The Times*, with the future in mind wrote:

> She is always in attendance on the battlefields to aid the wounded . . . I have seen her go down under fire with her little store of creature comforts for our wounded men and a more skilful hand about a wound or a broken limb could not be found among our best surgeons . . . I have witnessed her devotion and her courage; I have already borne testimony to her services to all who needed them . . . and I trust that England *will not forget* the one who nursed her sick and who sought out her wounded to aid and succour them and who performed the last office for some of her illustrious dead. [My italics]

In 1855, when the war ended, Florence Nightingale returned to Britain to national honours and public adulation. Mary Seacole on the other hand returned to Britain bankrupt and forgotten and died in Paddington in May 1881. She was buried in St Mary's Catholic Cemetery in Kensal Green. And white Britain suffered a traditionally convenient loss of memory.

It was no great leap in the dark when Asquith's government sent for what they considered to be their blacks and Asians. And to ensure that among black people slavery had not become just an idea, and also to make blacks and Asians admit, by their very presence on the battlefield, that they were still subject to white British control, they were included in Britain's Great War against Germany, to be used as guinea-pigs on the battlefield of Ypres. Or had the black and Asian peoples expected Independence in return for their wartime contribution? According to G. M. Trevelyan, author of *A Shortened History of England*, writing about the contribution of the white populations of Empire who also fought for Britain the mother country:

> When the war was over, each Dominion insisted on a full recognition of its nationhood. They claimed individual representation in the league of Nations, and the right to retain those German colonies they had themselves taken in the war. And finally, in 1931, the Statute of Westminster has given legal

force to the long-established custom that the Parliament of Great Britain should legislate for the Dominions only at their own request. Laws affecting the succession to the Crown can only be altered only with the concurrence of each of the Dominions, and the King can take no advice about appointments or other action in the Dominions except from Dominion Statesmen.

A magnificent reward. Canada had raised 650,000 men, New Zealand and Australia about 300,000 men each, and the whites got their way. The West Indies and black Africa contributed 135,000 men, and India had raised a force of one and a half million men and blacks and Indians got their traditional deserts. Nothing.

A reaction was not long in coming. India was angry. A storm of nationalist hostilities and political agitation against the continued British presence on Indian territory swept the sub-continent. Independence from Britain was their ambition. And Mahatma Ghandi would be its Messiah.

In Amritsar, British tempers scaled the heights after riots ended with the deaths of four or five British nationals, although many more Indians than whites died as a result of those riots. It was April 1919, and rumours of insurrection abounded, conjuring up inherited memories of a former pseudo-Indian Mutiny. A substantial reminder was needed, and Brigadier-General Reginald Dyer, CB, Britain's agent by proxy and her revengeful instrument of suppression, was the man.

At Jallianwalla Bagh, in the centre of Amritsar, on 13 April 1919, hundreds of Indians attending a banned political rally were the target. Like a nightmare, the demonstrators were surrounded by General Dyer's men, and they weren't out sightseeing. To make sure that his intentions were carried out with complete success an armoured car was also present.

The reality of their position struck home to the crowd when the soldiers fired point-blank into the brown mass of humanity for several minutes. The 'official' British figures for this act of supreme insanity was 379 dead with 1,500 wounded. Not surprisingly, the Indian figure was 800 dead with many more wounded. Amritsar would be an object lesson. And if the Indians, indeed, if any of Britain's colonized black and brown peoples ever needed a salutary reminder of their position in Britain's eyes, with a vengeance, Amritsar was it. But what was important was that the end of the Great War signified Britain's confused and abrupt arrival into the twentieth century, and the era of any black and Asian doubts pertaining to true British intentions had ended.

Even though a rebellion against Britain's political and military control at that time seemed impossible, some Africans tried it. A Britain at war, they felt, was a Britain off her guard. Nyasaland, now Malawi, was one such example. Reverend John Chilembwe was the black nationalist, and the misuse of blacks by Britain spearheaded his case. He published an article in November 1914, criticizing the forcing of black people to fight for Britain in the Great War. On 23 January 1915, he wrote to his men:

> This very night you are to go and strike the blow and then die ... This is the only way to show the whiteman that the treatment they are treating our men and women was most bad and we have decided to strike a first and a last blow, and then all die by the heavy storm of the whiteman's army. The whitemen will then think, after we are dead, that the treatment they are treating our people is almost bad, and they might change.
> [Quoted in James Morris's *Farewell the Trumpets*]

One fact is plainly obvious. Chilembwe knew that British firepower was superior to his own, but his resolve can be seen as an act of supreme frustration, to be equated with the reaction of Bristol's blacks in 1980 and Brixton's in 1981.

In those frustrating circumstances, the strength of the opposition is unimportant. Consequently, Chilembwe led an abortive revolt against British rule and white exploitation of blacks. The result was that Chilembwe was shot and his followers were hanged.

Dr Walter Rodney, author of *How Europe Underdeveloped Africa* (1972) wrote:

Sustenance given by colonies to the colonisers was most obvious and very decisive in the case of contributions by soldiers from among the colonised. Without colonial troops, there would have been no 'British forces' fighting on the Asian front in the 1939–45 war, because the ranks of the 'British forces' were filled with Indians and other colonials, including Africans and West Indians. It is a general characteristic of colonialism that the metropole utilised the manpower of the colonies. The Romans had used soldiers of one conquered nationality to conquer other nationalities, as well as to defend Rome against enemies. Britain applied this to Africa ever since the early 19th century, when the West Indian Regiment was sent across the Atlantic to protect British interests on the West African Coast. The West Indian Regiment had black men in the ranks, Irish (colonials) as NCO's, and Englishmen as officers. By the end of the 19th century, the West Indian Regiment included lots of Sierra Leoneans.

The most important force in the conquest of West African colonies by the British was the West African Frontier Force – the soldiers being Africans and the officers English. In 1894, it was joined by the West African Regiment, formed to help suppress the so-called 'Hut tax war' in Sierra Leone, which was the expression of widespread resistance against the imposition of colonial rule. In East and Central Africa, the King's African Rifles was the unit which tapped African fighting power on behalf of Britain. The African regiments supplemented military apparatus in several ways. Firstly, they were used as emergency forces to put down nationalist uprisings in the various colonies. Secondly, they were used to fight other Europeans inside Africa, notably during the first and second world wars. And thirdly, they were carried to European battlefields or to theatres of war outside Africa.

Furthermore, Indians under British orders fought against blacks. An example is given in the 1977 issue of *Africa Yearbook* published by *Africa Journal*, quoting the case of Nyasaland: 'In 1893, the name of the country was changed from Nyasaland Protectorate to the British Central African Protectorate. The country was finally "pacified" in 1897, with the help of Indian troops.'

With only 150 white landgrabbers in Nyasaland at that time, it is not surprising they used their colonized Indians to colonize the Africans. Furthermore, from *Africa Yearbook*:

> During the First World War, the country was invaded by German troops from Tanganyika. The Germans were repulsed and later Nyasaland became a base for British operations against German forces in East Africa. A total of 18,920 Nyasalanders were recruited for service with the King's African Rifles, and 191,200 rendered service as carriers and non-combatants.

Most significantly, Britain's military colonial practices had sown enmities among Asians, West Indians and Africans, by giving them a Roman holiday and U-turning them into exterminators of each other. An historic tool, as we shall see, to be used when those Asians, West Indians and Africans arrived to settle in Britain. It relied on completely ignoring their common denominators, while exploiting and accentuating any difference that could be found.

World War Two prophesied the severing of the life-line between Britain and her colonies, and the potential cutting of the master/servant Gordian knot. But all was not over just yet. Britain's scheming intention, for her black and Asian soldiers, was for them to remain passive when it suited her and aggressive whenever she so ordered.

Blacks and Asians were conscripted into World War Two, encouraged by hints of Independence as a reward when Britain's problems were over. But, as will be seen, the moment Britain had solved her problems of war, forgetfulness was the order of the day, and the relationship between her and her subject peoples would again revert to master and slave. But in this her greatest moment of crisis, she failed to notice the supposed inferiority of her 'inferior peoples', and thus she sowed the seed for future rebellion. The slaves who had fought for Britain in wartime would continue their fight for freedom against her in peace.

Nineteen forty-six heralded impending change, and dictatorship and/or Marxist philosophy became the new method of government for some emerging nations. Great Britain was no longer able to hold in abeyance the inevitable. In the process of annihilating her wartime enemies, like Germany, Italy and Japan, Britannia exposed herself. West Indians, Indians and Africans alike had witnessed that most Roman of all British institutions, the British Army, suffer significant reverses during World War Two. The myth of her might had been, in their eyes, laid low. Her grand illusion had crumbled when her subject peoples recognized the weak link in Britain's historically unbreakable chain.

Harold Macmillan once wrote that the British were 'masters of the world and heirs of the future'. But now the United States of America was very much in evidence, turning the Pax Britannica into the Pax Americana. And Britain became shackled by a myriad of homespun myths, legends, and memories and future heirs to trouble. The British Empire had reached its climax with Queen Victoria's Diamond Jubilee in 1897, and had been breaking apart ever since. The end was in sight. Great Britain had been the black man's burden, but the white man's burden was the stunning realization that he was being given orders, marching orders, and the commanders were black. Decolonization was the white man's Exodus.

Lord Curzon, Viceroy of India 1898–1905, had said:

As long as we rule India, we are the greatest power in the world. If we lose it we shall drop straight away to a third rate power . . . Your ports and your coaling stations, your fortresses and your dockyards, your Crown colonies and protectorates will go too. For either they will be unnecessary, or the tollgates and barbicans of an Empire that has vanished.

And so it was.

From the moment Britain evacuated India, her Empire was in a perpetual state of breaking apart by instalments, leaving in its wake an obstinate 'Empire mentality'. When Britain lost her imperial possessions, the sense of superiority subscribed to by whites over blacks and Asians continued, based on a now defunct power. And the time of sham began. Today, Britain's politicians in a cloud of bogus power continue to formulate foreign policies assuming that they still hold, internationally, yesterday's influence sponsored by yesterday's source of power.

Inside the British Empire mentality lies the idea that she has a meaningful say in today's world events, but in fact she does not; that at times of international crisis she commands an equal vote with the USA, Russia and China at the negotiating tables of power. That too is far from the truth. In fact, it would be overestimating the case to believe that the prospects of any human being outside Britain depended on the state of affairs in Britain today. Because that was not always the case, it is therefore a painful reality for many of Britain's whites who feel frustrated and uneasy when confronted by the staggering realization that world power is in the hands of the Americans, Russians and Chinese. And the decision as to whether Britain, on the world platform, moves this way or that, will be made in Washington, not London. From King and Queen to pawn.

The NATO Secretary General Dr Josef Luns warned in April 1981: 'I would take issue with the assumption that the less powerful members of the Alliance will be understanding if they are habitually excluded from deliberations bearing on their interests.' A statement based more on optimism than honesty. Dr Luns is well aware of the fact that within the history of the SALT negotiations, within the reality of international politics, policy on such issues has always been and will continue to be decided by America on behalf of the West, and the Soviet Union on behalf of the East. He would do well to remember that if America was not effectively the West's decider, he would not need to make such an unrealistic statement. Moreover, if the United States of America is determined to force European and British acceptance of the Cruise missile, or any other type of missile on their territories, America will succeed, and the British Empire mentality will have been dealt another wounding body blow.

Consequently, through the loss of her Empire, Great Britain has suffered continuous stinging reminders of the loss of her former global authority. But it was not until 1979 that the unfamiliar phrase 'negotiate not dictate' finally entered the British political vocabulary. It was Mrs Thatcher the new Prime Minister, thinking of her new charge as an imperial power, who made the mistake. Her statement, made in Canberra, Australia, helped change a few white ideas about using bully-boy tactics on blacks. Mrs Thatcher, hypocritically labelled the Iron Lady by the Russians, while lecturing a press conference said that she was ready to grant recognition to the lurching regime of Bishop Muzorewa, the great white hope, and Ian Smith, the promised-land leader. And to lift – unilaterally – the mandatory UN sanctions.

According to the *Guardian* columnist, Patrick Keatley, in March 1981, the black reaction to her Canberra statement was totally unexpected. He wrote:

> Total British exports to Nigeria had topped the £1,000 million mark by 1977 and reached £1,133 million the next year. Then came a setback, in which the largest factor was political. Hasty statements by the incoming Thatcher administration brought the overnight decision to nationalize the assets of BP in Nigeria. It was a warning shot to show that Nigeria would not idly tolerate a handover to white minority rule in Rhodesia.

The result was, in recognizing economic reality, Mrs Thatcher backed down and, in doing so, the British Lion was de-fanged and de-clawed. Nigeria, over this issue, represented the international black spirit, the jagged piece of glass stuck in the intestinal tract of white Britain.

It is a fact that Ian Smith declared UDI on 11 November 1965. It is also a fact that successive British governments did nothing about that illegal declaration. Furthermore, black people with their white allies fought against both the illegal white administration in Salisbury and against the racist inactiveness of Britain's governments. But the reality is that Zimbabwe's blacks were and still are the majority. Therefore, power by political definition is rightly theirs. In recognition of that white-frightening fundamental, Robert Mugabe, the so-called black terrorist, became Prime Minister of Zimbabwe, *persona grata* for the black majority and their white allies.

The grand sham continues. One would have thought the moment of decolonization was a glorious moment for the United Kingdom to seek new directions and fresh beginnings. But that was not so. It took several years, with a little help from vociferous black and Asian leaders, for Britain's politicians to recognize that *their* British Commonwealth, was not in fact British, but international. Or was the British Commonwealth another form of Empire on the cheap?

Nevertheless, the British Commonwealth gave way to The Commonwealth. And Britons finally settled for an imperial illusion through the continuance of imperial titles. The OBE (Order of the British Empire) and the MBE (Member of the British Empire), conferred while the Empire was still alive, continue to be bestowed. Or are the OBE and the MBE and other such imperial memorabilia still in existence in order to remind the nostalgic British that there had been an Empire?

Europe too became aware of the loss of British power and colonial trading market, through the public death of her Empire. It took ten years and many attempts before Britain was accepted into the European Economic Community. General de Gaulle's veto may have reflected that loss as well as a reluctance to accept France's traditional competitor into an organization in which France was pre-eminent. That there was anyone bold enough to humiliate Britannia without retribution was unthinkable. But there was, and de Gaulle was such a man.

There were conditions attached to her entry into the EEC. Conditions dictated by some members of the Community, principally France and Germany. It was because of those unacceptable conditions that she found it necessary to re-negotiate the Treaty of Rome after her entry into the EEC, twice.

For Britons, this was a case of chickens coming home to roost. There had been a time when it would have been Britain who decided whether to create an EEC, or not. Britain also would have decided which European countries could become members. Most significantly, she would have dictated policy for such an august body, if necessary through her customary methods of gunboat diplomacy. But those days were over. Now here was Britain being dictated to by her rival, France.

Britannia's distress was that her power belonged to another era, and here in 1973 it was a new one; where no amount of bygone power could strengthen her obvious powerlessness. Britain could not dictate, but had to negotiate, from a position of economic weakness. Neither the status nor the energy could be found to counter the confidence of some Common Market countries who were negotiating from a position of economic strength. And In Place of Strife was More Strife to come.

Observed from a black or Asian position, it is an Empire mentality which compels Britain's blacks and Asians to exist in a white world of intolerance, injustice, unemployment to an extreme, and continuous ill-treatment. They are not welcome but merely tolerated on British soil. But white intolerance continuously sharpens the ideas of black and Asian people. And brains honed to determination through necessity, heavily aided by racial injustice, are trembling potentials for spontaneous or purposeful rebellion at any moment. British television as a devil's disciple plays its part by constantly reminding blacks and Asians what they will never be, i.e. equal, and what they will never have, i.e. status. So pressures continue to build, for, to be reasonable in the alienated reserves of the Brixtons of Britain is tough. If conditions do not change, and soon, for black and Asian people, and if white men continue to rule through imperial attitudes, with illusions of racial pre-eminence, blacks and Asians living in Britain will prove to be the most costly of Britannia's imperial acquisitions.

Bishop Colin O'Brien Winter captured the essence of white treatment of black and Asian people living in Britain in his foreword to John Downing's publication *Now You Do Know*, published in 1980. He wrote:

Aneurin Bevan, ex-miner and M.P., once warned Winston Churchill in a memorable speech in the House of Commons, 'not to wince before the lash falls'. John Downing's report falls like a lash on the smug, the silent, the unconvinced and the uncaring people of Britain who either pretend that there is no racial prejudice in this country, or ignore the massive injustice, the daily violence and the sufferings that black people undergo. The author, in his preface, feels no hope that the mass of people here will face up to, let alone act on, the appalling reality of the racism that exists here and, because of this, he aims his report at the wider international readership. One is immediately reminded of the situation that pertained in Germany after the war with Hitler, when the overwhelming mass of the German people, having failed to challenge Hitler's murderous policies, tried to excuse their silence by pleading ignorance to what was going on in their country. The rest of the world judged them guilty of being accomplices to Hitler's atrocities against the Jews, adding that silence in such situations was tantamount to complicity. After reading this report, I am even more convinced that we in Britain are, for the most part, accomplices in the injustices suffered by black people here and that outside world opinion will condemn us for our appalling silence and our cold-hearted indifference to the racism that we harbour uncritically in our personal as well as national life . . .

Drawing on researched statistics, the writer shows that racism repeatedly goes unchecked and unchallenged as far as attitudes to the overwhelming majority of blacks are concerned. When racism is exposed, as it is from time to time, white society prefers evasions, cover ups and excuses.

The 'cover ups' mentioned by Bishop Winter are the sweeping of nasty actualities, like colour discrimination, under a carpet of innocence. For instance, under the guise of 'doing their duty', some members of the British police force practise barefaced racism through a device known as the 'Sus charge'. Alternatively known as Section 4 of the 1824 Vagrancy Act, it was conceived to deal with Irish settlers seeking refuge from the Irish Potato famine and thousands of demobilized soldiers and sailors home from the Napoleonic wars. The end result was that huge numbers of able bodied men roamed the country looking for work, often while starving. For Lord Liverpool's government this was a situation which called for drastic measures. In came the Vagrancy Act, making it a criminal offence to be without a visible means of support. It also gave a police constable the power to arrest a person whom the constable suspected of being *about to commit* a crime; along with the power to arrest a tramp, a reputed thief, an idle or disorderly person (known in law as rogues and vagabonds respectively), an incorrigible rogue and fortune tellers. In reality, it amounted to the arrest of anyone the constable did not like the look of. Which really meant that anybody who did not have a clearly defined position in British society, or no fixed address and no acceptable means of earning a living, was fair game. But the Vagrancy Act of 1824 was scarcely enforced because at that time there were literally no policemen. As a result the fortune tellers and now unemployed ex-soldiers were not gravely harassed. For example, in the town of Oldham, Lancashire, with an 1820 population of 60,000, there was no resident magistrate and no effective force of law and order. Had there been people guilty of contravening the Vagrancy Act they would have escaped detention. There was nobody capable of effecting an arrest. In London also, there were no police, but there were Bow Street Runners. They were nothing more than a bunch of thieves licensed by magistrates to carry on their trades providing the magistrate received a percentage of their ill-gotten gains.

Two developments solved the problem. Firstly, Britain's economic improvement at the end of the 1840 drastically reduced the number of unemployed and, secondly, Sir Robert Peel's creation of a police force, a disciplined body of uniformed constables who patrolled the streets. Prevention by presence had arrived.

But Britain's black community in the 1960s and 70s, with its increasing number of able-bodied unemployed, has fallen victim as no other group ever before to the incredibly loosely defined power vested in the Vagrancy Act. An Act which is being used by many whites in uniform as a stick to beat those whom the white population has shown its dislike and fear of.

The prime minority white legal objection to the Vagrancy Act is that the evidence consists solely of the uncorroborated word of police officers who themselves must justify the arrests they have made. To grant an acquittal, the magistrate must say that he does not believe police evidence. Ignoring any bias that may exist on the part of the magistrate against the type of defendants concerned, disbelief of police evidence, under this law, in practice rarely happens. Thus effectively the police can lay a charge on a person with near certainty of its success, relying solely on their own unsubstantiated evidence. No victim and no material evidence need be produced. In practice no evidence is ever produced, apart from notebooks.

The prime objection of the black community to the Vagrancy Act comes in two stages. Firstly, the black community agrees with the minority legal objection. And secondly, in Britain's two-tiered society of black and white, where the interpretation of the law is two-faced, a law which gives *carte blanche* to white policemen who use white paranoia as a yardstick, invites itself to be misused, in order to obtain an easy conviction. Politically, in the wake of the white racial insurgency against blacks, the Vagrancy Act by its obvious misuse is nothing other than an instrument of repression. Of all the youths charged under the Vagrancy Act in 1977, forty-two per cent were black. As all blacks in Britain (minus Asians) numbered under one million, out of a fifty-six million white population, forty-two per cent is a high proportion of guaranteed success. So white dismissal of the cries of unfair treatment is another racial cover up.

But the largest white betrayal of all, being the most subtle, is openly practised in the run-up to a general election.

Election time, a time when issues are the currency of the language of politics. A time when the electorate is licensed to kill the government, and the issue is the provoking agent on which the government either retains power, or falls. The polling station, custodian of the nation's ability and right for peaceful change, on polling day is filled with voters, each carrying a holdall of national colics: inflation, unemployment, law and order, reduction of income tax, housing, education, health services, etc. And the prospective candidate, as a constituent instrument of the people's will, while promising change itself, will become the reason why an issue, locally or nationally, arises at the next election.

Ever since the Commonwealth Immigrants Act was helped onto the statute books in 1962, by a phalanx of Aryan evangelists, The Issue for blacks and Asians at every general election since then has been immigration. Whole communities look on in horror as this issue is opportunistically manipulated by candidates seeking a white majority vote. At those elections, the polling booth holdalls carried by many white voters also hold all that is uppermost in their minds, which is the fresh crop of racial resentment they carry as a guilty secret and, clinging to deep-rooted fears of racial impurity manipulated out at the dawn before *the* day by negrophobic sermonizers on the street and in the media, they dangerously intertwine their racial animosities with the privilege of the vote, and their guilty secret can finally be freed inside the covered-up secrecy of the polling booth. They vote from fear, in reaction and in haste; inside the booth where honesty, however dishonest, will prove their choice right or wrong for anything up to five years.

Nevertheless, it is a powerfully horrific feast for the eyes to witness so many of the so-called 'ethnic minorities' (blacks and Asians) bad mouthed and stamped upon, accompanied by the animosities of Britain's whites, for having come to Britain in search of anything. Those whites must sneer in the run-up period to a general election: after the black and Asian experience of centuries of white oppression in yesteryear's colonies, what did you black and Asian people expect to receive in the heart of racism itself? Or did you really believe that the cancer of injustice was only practised in your own countries by a minority of Britain's whites? Did you believe that the long-drawn anguish of watching your people being crucified, physically and spiritually, would be ended on Britannia's soil?

After 1950, Britain's black and Asian white-house contract with convertible terms was given an extension clause. Traditionally, their life-function had been to help Britain's whites achieve their obsessive deep-rooted ambitions in the West Indies, Africa and Asia. And that in-house duty had been to create a comfortable downy life in the sun for the colonial whites. It is true that Britain's colonial whites drew up the plans for technological advances – mostly to suit white purposes – but it is just as true that the physical and economically profitable side of Britannia's colonial enterprises was only achieved through the blood, sweat and tears of black and Asian labourers who received a tenth of the reward Britain's whites gave themselves.

However, because of white Britain's post-war labour necessity, blacks and Asians were still required to fulfil their traditional white-house duty, but now it was extended to help create a comfortable downy life for Britain's whites in Britain itself.

British attitudes have scarcely progressed since the following article appeared in volume 34 of *The Gentleman's Magazine* in 1764. At that time there existed 20,000 black servants out of a total London population of 676,250. And true to white belief in the sub-humanity of blacks, the inoculation of cattle was discussed in the same article. The article said:

> The practice of importing Negro servants into these Kingdoms is said to be already a grievance that requires a remedy, and yet it is everyday encouraged, insomuch that the number in this metropolis only, is supposed to be near 20,000; the main objection to their importation is, that they cease to consider themselves as slaves in this free country, nor will they put up with an inequality of treatment, nor more willingly perform the laborious offices of servitude than our own people, and if put to do it, are generally sullen, spiteful, treacherous, and revengeful. It is therefore highly impolitic to introduce them as servants here, where that rigour and severity is impracticable which is absolutely necessary to make them useful.
>
> The mortality among the horned cattle rages in *Saxony* to a terrible degree. Insoculation has been practised in other countries with success, and is recommended to the sufferers there as the most effectual means to prevent the loss of their herds.

The white 1764 opinion of how black people will not 'put up with an inequality of treatment, nor more willingly perform the laborious offices of servitude than our own people,' is an opinion which nearly every black and Asian woman, man and child knows, in 1981, is subscribed to by the majority of Britain's whites. Furthermore, 'that they cease to consider themselves as slaves in this free country,' is a fundamental Britannic Race Law. But few if any of Britain's black and Asian immigrants in the 1950s would have heard or read about the 1760s white opinion of black people. But they would soon know what that old opinion felt like in modern-day Britain.

The great white father needed BPE (black people's effort). And out went an ulcerated 'come and help' Pied Piper-type invitation. A sasine invitation *comme il faut*. Britain had discovered that her blacks and Asians having also helped her to win her wars, were multi-purpose, and at this moment she considered that they came in handy. In much the same way as the people of Hamelin town, when they called for help to rid their town of an infestation of multi-coloured rats, the Pied Piper answered. But what Britain's invited minorities had not taken into account, in a glorious moment of impetuosity, was that when they had achieved their Britannic mission they, like the Pied Piper, would have outlived their usefulness. Interestingly, the Pied Piper with encouragement from Hamelin town council, left Hamelin town empty-handed. And the treacherous citizens of that town, much to their surprise, lost out as well.

Britain was advertised as a promised land, through the circulation of postcards, brochures and posters of the more pleasant scenes. She had a plethora of schools and bustled with trade and commerce; there were scenes of London and its busy happy markets, its Mall, St James's Park and Trafalgar Square, crowded with a host of quaint two-storey lorries called double-deckers; streets in a figurative sense were paved with gold. This all reinforced the black and Asian belief that living conditions, employment and educational opportunities in Britain were literally fantastic. Through all this visual feasting, many British-bound blacks and Asian travellers began to develop a mother-country world-of-fantasy with the hope they saw in their much-trumpeted El Dorado come-to-Britain invitations.

And together with the rest of the white Empire they had sung the imperial belief: Land of hope and glory, mother of the free. How shall we extol thee who art born of thee? The traditional white answer to that question for blacks was: work, work and more work. But little did the hopeful blacks and Asians realize that their invitations carried with them a time-bomb, tick, tick, tick, slowly and inexorably ticking towards a racial crescendo, and more so towards the truth, which was: 'We don't want you to breed your children here, we don't really want you to settle here, but we won't say so at this moment because then you may not come – Your Country Needs You.'

Necessity being the mother of invention, white necessity invented the *accidental blindness,* which prevented Britain's whites from seeing the racial, social and cultural threat they would suddenly see some years later. Superficially, the United Kingdom excreted a mirage of welcome. But in truth, she was a regurgitating Venus fly-trap energized by alternating racial currents.

So into Britain came the new settlers, an assortment of people with their different magical hues, ignorant of the secret that they were really 'guest workers'. They came to feed her production lines, the ultimate hippodrome of inferiority in the testing ground of British class division; to feed her factories, fill her filthiest occupations and ultimately to be shot at like marbles from all sides of the ring. They had arrived to take their place on the Arctic side of Britain's streets without complaint, to work as postmen, counter clerks, sorters, cleaners, messengers, porters, sweepers, on the buses as conductors and drivers and on the railways. They worked for anyone who would employ them and for wages so low that even those whites who considered themselves from the wrong side of the tracks refused to inherit the indignity of accepting wages accepted by blacks and Asians. By their very presence in Britain they had unknowingly elevated people whom the white upper and middle classes had always considered, by birth and by treatment, along with their perpetual acceptance of that negative treatment, to be the white niggers of Britain. They accepted treatment which had hitherto been reserved for the 'lowest' whites, and the workplace, the schools, the streets, working-men's and other clubs and their houses were turned into an arena, a racial testing ground. This drives one to ask, does the moral life of Britain incorporate any truth? Or is Britain's truth the following passage, gleaned from the inviting pages of *Going to Britain*? published by the British Broadcasting Corporation for West Indians en route to the United Kingdom in the 1950s:

Making Friends

Going to church is not likely to help you find a better room to live or a job. The people may have much the same problem as yourself and in any case they do not attend church to find someone they can help. Their presence in church, like yours, is no evidence of sainthood. If they smile with you in church and look away from your direction in the bus, it is just one of those things and you are free to do the same.

However, the friend you make at church will tend to be more sincere than those made – say at the pub, for instance, or dance hall. People will grow to respect you a little more if they see you often in the church. Sometimes they decide to give you credit for being truly converted, and then they expect big things from you simply because they may have it in their heads that coloured people are heathens who break the hearts of saintly missionaries who try to convert them.

But whatever people think, the church remains a good place to go. You may find friends there – you almost certainly will – but, if you don't, you can get there a truer picture of what you are really up against.

But there is another aspect of British truth which can be seen in the following passages from the same booklet, which encourage the then immigrant settlers to accept white antagonism:

You are the Stranger

However, your greater problem will be getting on with your white neighbours. One thing you must always keep in mind, is that their knowledge of your country is much less than your knowledge of theirs. Whenever you are inclined to get angry or fly off the handle at some remark – or because a person stares at you for a long time – remember that English people are ignorant of your ways and habits, and they may be just displaying a natural curiosity. There are some parts of England where the sight of a coloured man is still an uncommon thing, and there are people who may never have seen a person like you before . . .

No Offence Meant

Don't take offence at things like these. If, in the house you live, you see one or two of them whispering and pointing to you, it may well be that they are wondering why you wear your hat with the brim turned up all around, for instance, it doesn't have to mean that they are making fun of you. And where you find a healthy curiosity, it will pay you to go out of your way to explain things to them. You may be surprised at some of the questions they may ask you, and you might feel they are insulting you on the sly, but it is only their ignorance of you and your country . . .

Politeness the Key

. . . They don't stand on the doorstep gossiping, or form a crowd on the pavement to talk about the latest ballad. I notice some West Indians still have that habit and I can tell you it isn't one that English people like. What they like is politeness.

In those passages from the BBC's introduction to Britain, lies an obvious – to whites only – respect for the intelligence of Britain's black settlers. That *is* the truth, along with that other forgotten truth which was proven during Britain's slave trade, and again inside her colonies; and which was, with the influx of Britain's black and Asian settlers, about to be proved yet again. That is the internationally recognized assertion that everyone has rights which include responsibilities. But what blacks and Asians, side by side with their white allies, have long held to be universally axiomatic, is that in a world dominated by white power structures, it is the whites who have the rights, while everyone else bears the responsibilities for white actions. It is clear from the quoted passages from *Going to Britain?* that black people *were again asked* to bear the responsibility for white behaviour.

Consequently, it was not long before the Chapeltowns, the Bradfords, the Handsworths, the Smethwicks, the Southalls, the Notting Hills and the Brixtons of Britain became synonymous with black or Asian. It took even less time for many white *tourists* to see into those places and pronounce them to be third-rate, places where failures lived. And it only took a glance to realize that everywhere else sported 'Coloureds Need Not Apply' signs. A Few did apply without success, but most gave up. You could see the 'No Coloureds' notices everywhere, for jobs, flats, bedsits and many hotels. There were many places which avoided advertising their racial hang-ups, and had no notices. They allowed a black person to enter, but the temperature of the frost-biting atmosphere told them to go elsewhere. So black people kept to themselves and so did the Asians. Consequently, Britain's inner city police forces, by virtue of the black closed-shop, encouraged and strengthened by white race-conscious fellow travellers, did not immediately discover that it is virtually impossible to effectively police a white-antagonized and therefore antagonistic black society made secret by white racism. Where should they start? Obviously somewhere easy. On the streets? Is that why there has been a plethora of young black 'Sus' arrests under the Vagrancy Act of 1824?

In the 1950s, there were few whites who knew or could even hazard a guess as to what blacks or Asians did after leaving work. Of course, out of sight was out of mind. What whites did not see, if it happened to blacks, did not happen at all. Moreover, what all blacks and all Asians had in common, as per their lot, was to live inside white men's generalizations; simply because according to those generalizations, they were a stagnant people, brainless and changeless. Anything could and did happen to those types of people.

You could see black and brown men and women, some of whom were highly qualified, with university degrees, working on the underground and buses, cleaning faeces off hospital beds and floors, and, as I did, feeding J. Lyons kitchens with their labour. Sure, white people did those jobs as well, but at that time that is all black and Asian people ever did.

Amid the moral pollution that insufficiency sponsors, you could perceive these settlers constantly seeking ways out of their overcrowded, damp and often dank and lightless abodes. Occasionally somewhere was found, usually a mirage where there were no NO COLOUREDS notices in evidence, but the price for these scarce 'glad pads' for blacks and Asians was a doubled rent.

The moral crucifixion of black and Asian people began the day they landed on British soil. Those were the days when white men behaved (though many still do) as if they, individually, had had a hand in admitting black and Asian people into Britain. The new settlers, in return, were supposed to behave gratefully to each and every white man. Therefore, each new settler started life in Britain three steps behind a white. One, he was not white. Two, he had to be grateful for being here. And three, he had to be grateful to each white individual for having allowed him in, so he must say wonderful things about Britain to justify his entry and his presence in Britain. The gospel of hundreds of thousands of great white fathers was refurbished. Advice usually given to their English rose-complexioned, slender and sensitive young daughters when travelling abroad was changed from 'Beware of Men in the Tropics' to 'Beware of Tropical Men'.

A generation grew up watching the humiliation and degradation heaped onto the heads of their parents, which they accepted with little complaint to white authority. Who could they complain to, and who would listen? It was also a time when other blacks turned away in shame if another black fell into an argument with a white. It was an era when to become involved in that argument might result in those whites who had a grudge against life, pointing accusingly with what became their standard black put-down, 'You have a chip on your shoulder', even though they seemed to be the only ones who could see it. It was a moment when the best way to avoid that accusation, even though it was meaningless, was to admit white right with black silence. Therefore, any black who defended him or herself was automatically labelled a troublemaker.

So a generation grew up knowing full well that what was happening to them was morally, spiritually, politically and humanly, wrong. Their parents' apparent crime was that they did not *en masse* protest hard enough. But maybe they had other things like being grateful, plus making a living for their families and creating opportunities for their children, plus *knowing* that they would never rise above the street, on their minds.

For a moment, black and Asian people lived in Britain inside their white stereotype, in order to lessen the racist pressure on their skulls. For a moment, their silence, through continuous white dismissals of their many grievances, was deafening. For another moment, Britain's whites, in a racial sense, had never had it so good through having it all their own way. They had, temporarily, succeeded in relegating blacks and Asians to Meanwhile Alley.

Meanwhile, Mayfair and the more salubrious areas of London and other cities and all the places where blacks and Asians were never seen, were (and still are) the white man's gilded paradise. Whereas the Southalls and Brixtons of Britain were the blacks' and browns' exotically depressing shanty towns. Seen through white eyes, they were (and still are), human zoos on a grand scale, filled with prehistoric relics and, being out on a limb, they became the stamping grounds of otherwise unemployable white sociologists; along with racially-opportunistic bored middle-class whites who drove down to these zoos for their 'good times' while playing with and observing the ways of the relics. There were Oxbridge 'Leakeys' brushing up on their zoological studies being towed along by snappily-dressed musical burglars who plundered black rhythm by ear; accompanied by an advance guard of rebelling Hooray Henrys tearing down the beaten track just to try it black or brown; closely followed up by God's servants relieving their guilt by trying to clear up the Britannic mess. They were all prancing across the foreign but British L. S. Lowry tenement-scape, mouthing anachronisms: 'You people are such good dancers, and we bet you're good in bed. We bet you're good at running, but you don't have much in your heads.' It was, I suppose, the black and brown inauguration into the cultivated life of Britain.

None the less, these 'zoos' were seen by whites as the lands of darkness. As far as blacks were concerned, they were places where whites' conjured-up-and-conditioned ideas of black people happened. Where they spent all day sleeping and eating smelly food, all night partying, revelling, and leaping on loose white women while making their living trafficking in drugs. According to that charitable mentality, the Asians were just as guilty by keeping themselves to themselves: 'Goodness knows what they get up to without us.' A reflection on the white state of mind?

These things, somewhere at sometime, may have happened, as surely as they could also happen and probably did, inside white society. What is much more likely to be closer to the truth is that other things happened as well. Like work, like ignoring white racist attacks, like aspiring, like creating for themselves a stable community where their children could use the few opportunities their parents were giving them, like disregarding KBW (Keep Britain White), Wogs Out, Niggers Go Home and other racist graffiti. Like chasing illusive jobs by residing at the Labour

Exchange; like trying to find better accommodation, or just finding accommodation; like contributing to Britain's economy and hence its society. It was that kind of activity black and Asian people were involved in and which white society did its best to disregard. For those whites, black effort did not exist. But with the obvious and often blatant animosity toward the black and Asian newcomers, the burning question was: had white Britain finally lost her innocence of racism? She had lost it, brutally, several centuries ago, but with the presence of black and brown aliens on her much-coveted pleasant pastures, she was *now* beginning to notice. And it hurt.

Britain hurt too. Walking through the crumbling ghettos where despair and dejection hung about in groups on lonely sidewalks, you could see them treading water in the shadows on the beat each night. These streets were full of hunters and the haunted. And the hot jazz of high-powered discrimination blew loud and clear into a growing mountain of determination emitting the soul chorus, 'Keep the faith, baby'. Some would, some wouldn't. While the in-betweens just mouthed disbelief at the audaciousness and blatancy of white Britain's racial nepotism. I am making the scene. This is the main drag of many tears. This is Brixton. This is Southall. This is Chapeltown. This is Handsworth. This is Powis Square. This is Babylon. This is anywhere. And the whites are somewhere else. Lost in Britannic pride.

Hope in white Britain for blacks and Asians was, and still is, a frail and delicious ordeal. Whereas hope, in the black and brown sense in the 1950s and 1960s, was summed up on the lips of nearly every black and Asian human being with the words, 'When I Go Back Home'. They had yet to realize that their British-born children (a parent's hope) might one day ask the shock questions, 'Where is home?' and 'Where is *our* hope?' and 'What is hope?' But those same children soon realized that life in Britain for them would be one long disenchantment, through the heavy news that being black or brown (or old, mentally handicapped or poor, or . . .) in Britain, is a crime.

Racism is moral in a racist country. At the very least, Britain's new settlers refused to accept that Britannic truth. For if you cannot refuse, you cannot control your past, present or future.

Making us cognizant of the fact that blacks and Asians living in Britain have always lived, and continue to live, inside a white fabrication of reality; even though the spaces in between their facts is the reality of their senses. An intrinsic truth few white men will ever know or understand.

The facts on each of us are the details which other people might read about us, usually from files or media reports. But reality is You, which the world will never really know or understand how you experience experience. Human experience is the pain, love, lust and happiness of human existence. And only You will ever really know what it smells like, looks like, tastes like, sounds like and feels like. My reality is politically, morally, spiritually, humanly and realistically, black. And so are the others, who grasped that in being considered Britain's social liabilities by her whites, their colour-talk blew out the afterglow of previous optimism in Britain with, 'Look here sisters and brothers, we have a white problem over here'.

It is almost impossible to be an individual in any country. But when the victimizing civilization of Britain is determined, in almost every way, to stop you from being somebody, that kind of mistake can be measured in terms of human misery. What happens then? Things get shattered into another plane and, so do people.

By 1958 black people had grown tired of being kicked in the face for being black. They reacted by fighting back and a minor race battle, known here as the Notting Hill *riots* (sic), blew the white breeze of racial resentment into a black storm of anger.

Daily Mirror columnist Keith Waterhouse, on 8 September 1958, had *the* answer and wrote:

> Who – or what – is behind the race riots?
>
> IGNORANCE is the real villain. Ignorance of how people live. Ignorance of their aims and their ambitions. Ignorance of what they are actually doing. Ignorance breeds fear. Fear breeds violence. The enemy of fear is FACT . . .
>
> . . . Today – meet the West Africans . . . WHO ARE THEY? GHANA – known until recently as the Gold Coast – is an independent country, equal in the Commonwealth with Australia, Canada and New Zealand. It has its own Prime

Minister and its own Parliament.

That then is a white definition of being civilized. What makes those blacks *not* savages, in this case, is the possession of a form of government recognizable, by virtue of its Westminster similarity, to whites. It is that simple. Or is it? What happens when the facts do not tally (they never do) with the white-preferred traditional fiction of black and Asian people? The history of the oppression of blacks and Asians by whites continues.

It is tantalizing to say that the 1958 Notting Hill *fracas* was straightforwardly due to white ignorance of black people. That the black Eddie Cochran was slain because the white who dusted his life away did so because he was ignorant of how Eddie lived, ignorant of his ambitions and ignorant of the fact that he was a human being. Or did his black colour disguise his humanity to his white assailant, who accidentally thought that he was butchering a sub-human species? Had he not, somewhere at sometime, read or heard of how many other British whites had also decided centuries ago, that wasting away black and Asian lives without retribution was acceptable to the white-erected system in Britain's colonial territories? Had he not watched his fellow whites' lack of interest which greeted the news of any slaying of a black by a white, even on Britain's streets?

What Keith Waterhouse – along with those other cliché-riding media men who perpetually use public ignorance as an excuse for unpalatable and unexplainable (by them) situations – forgot to mention, was that white ignorance of black and Asian facts is a white way of life and has always been so. The facts even when *known* to whites generally, are not merely dismissed, but are genetically forgotten. They *really* forget.

Consequently, there exists in Britain no real majority white interest in knowing the facts about black and Asian people. Thus the basis of Keith Waterhouse's identification of ignorance as the cause of the 1958 Notting Hill *riots* is ignorance. His own, along with the others. Equality for blacks and Asians was a long time coming, but the reaction of Britain's whites to blacks who stood up for themselves against racism, was not.

The answer to the black and Asian presence in Britain, to the white fear of that presence, the answer to blacks who complained when they had no right to, the answer to the black refusal to accept their negative white definition, the answer to black questions as to why they should accept second-best, in everything, why they should be overjoyed to see 'Coloureds Need Not Apply' notices, why they should be grateful, why they must accept the blame for Britain's economic, housing and unemployment problems, the answer to Notting Hill 1958, the answer to white ignorance through fear was the answer to racism. The answer was to *legitimize racism.*

The field was still in play, the referee blew his whistle and the rules were changed. The 1962 Commonwealth Immigrants Act was spawned and qualifications were required of blacks and Asians to enter the Britannic Kingdom of Heaven. Up on Lavender Hill, the day the Act was passed, a white man of octogenarian years with kindly eyes looked at me while I was reading a 'NO COLOUREDS' advert, noticed the anger splattered across my face and said: 'If you are shooting at us in twenty years' time, it will be because we put the gun in your hand, today.'

4
On the Brink

Yes, God does move in a mysterious way, and He has left many people confused. For what is freedom's price in this ugly experience?

Britannia has a rigid caste system, where the *right*-birth people by virtue of their birthright stay at the top, through fair means or foul. And the working-class masses, the leftovers, have been over the centuries buffeted and pummelled into dough, to await orders from above, the star commandment being, 'promise you won't do anything rash, like demanding your rights'. *Ad infinitum*. Into this social conspiracy, with Establishment backing, crawling with clues, the middle-class mass-market media evaporates the best verbal gun-bearers, through a system of reward or punishment, leaving the working-classes without incentive to rebel and leaderless. In Britain, ages ago, moral standards fell when there was a greater need – the profit motive – a greater competition; and the pulverized masses became the cheated debris of industrialized society. But truth, in its plain wrappings, became a delicate suffering, a modern-day luxury the ruling class could never afford; in dread, now, of granting anything for fear of losing everything, for fear of losing control. *Carpe diem*. They had practised a different form of democracy, alien to the theories of its Greek creators. Yes, the workers travelled on complacently, sabotaged by their own docility; enviously frustrated by the cakes-of-opportunity for the upper classes; highlighted in the present-day working-class conversational anathema, Britain's social separator: the public school for the privileged, private schools for the pretentious, standing an experience away from the comprehensive, comprehensively under-educating. Until a collection of black and brown Freedom Riders slipped onto the scene and the working classes ascended an experience closer to the middle classes. They were 'allowed' to, as a reward for having continued to 'see' *reason*, as a body politic, in their unreasonable lowly position. These Freedom Riders cultured in at the now vacant position, the bottom. The Britannic multi-racial body politic was complete, with its black and brown, potentially energetic, political scapegoats. Immediately, the counterfeit rumour, with *bona fides* attached, was sent abroad by upper and middle classes; announcing that, 'the class system has broken down; there is no such thing, no such animal called class, alive in Britain today'. Some believed it, some didn't. Some through apathetic insularity did not care. *The* grand Britannic fantasy; for in naked class terms, due to the titanium-like rigidity of the British class structure, past is the same as the present and presently will be the future.

A variety of exotic Freedom Riders perceived a Britannic factory class-triumvirate over them, each layer supportive of and dependent on the other. And those foreign bodies could see the differences, the lines of social division, between the haves, the have-nots and the never-will-haves; who *now* have a grudge against life, a grudge against everything, a grudge against foreign bodies, whom *all* whites tagged with one negative label after another, ending with, care of Scotland Yard's Labelling Department, 'Muggers'. There were lies and counter-lies and a geometric progression of exaggerations. The blacks and Asians were given 'walking papers' in the form of forced and then voluntary repatriation with much love from the management and staff of a depreciating Great Britain. Hey fellas, we've arrived. Or have we? Or are the foreign bodies half a stretch away from a new and more venomous insurgency?

White people said, 'you have no grievances'. Bristol 1980 said, 'we have'. White people said, 'Bristol was an isolated incident'. Brixton 1981 said, 'it wasn't'. White people said, 'you have no just causes'. Petrol bombs that burned alive entire Asian families, Asian youths stabbed to death in British streets and the New Cross Fire Massacre 1981, proved they did. White people said, '*you* have nothing to worry about'. Southall 1981 said, '*we* do'. The Great British Establishment (GBE) said, 'it's all the fault of the blacks'. Liverpool 1981 proved that class was involved. The GBE said, 'extremists have damaged race relations in Britain'. What relations? Or is what we have in Britain, today, what most people consider relationships should be like? I ask again. What *is* freedom's price in this ugly experience? It's the well-being of our children, the well-being of our sanity, the well-being of our next generation, the well-being of ourselves. Or is it?

In June 1977, I wrote an article for *New Society* about the well-being of our society and ourselves. Under the section 'Society at Work', *New Society* headlined it 'It couldn't happen here'. It stated:

Since this time last year, when massive police presence elevated the Notting Hill street festival/brawl into the status of a riot, tensions in London and the United Kingdom seem to have relaxed. The black *revolution*, on the surface, has relapsed into its traditional, characteristic inactivity. The over-enthusiastic tribes have been put down. Jolly good show. What threatened to become a disruption, appears once again to be manageable as a problem. Praise be de Lawd.

Of course, the dark mutterings of discontent go on: racism, oppression, lack of opportunity, bad housing and so on and so on. These institutionalized grumblings have become a necessary part of normal life. And that other part of normal life, the painful and bloody saga of Northern Ireland, continues.

A logical development of the increasing violence and bitterness of the Anglo/Irish fracas is the emergence and daily reinforcement of no go areas. This is not confined to Ireland. It happens here (and has been happening for some time) in areas of black/white aggression, Brixton and Southall for instance.

It is often said that the racial problems of America could never happen here. A statement based more on English optimism than political honesty. For example, Brixton, Harlesden, Willesden, Southall, Brick Lane E1, Kensal Rise and so on are London's Harlems. What could not happen is already here. Considering the many difficulties of the black and Asian minorities, it should be no surprise if the same attitudes emerge as are already apparent in the Irish militants.

Events show that there are two types of no go areas, with a third 'hospitably' advocated by the CRC. The first is where the whites cannot go, such as clubs and illegal shebeens. In the second, entry is not restricted – but nor is hostility. The third, which could be a potential no go, is the recommendation by the CRC that local authorities should 'encourage the growth' of all-black communities on council estates. But how are council bureaucrats, many of whom are distrusted by minorities, supposed to encourage? A Brixton shopkeeper from Guyana, John Mansfield, compared it with the Bantustans or homelands scheme of South Africa. 'Blacks,' he feels, could be 'placed on the worst estates' and most significantly 'we would be surrounded'. This apparent fear is a real one amongst many blacks.

There are incidents which those professing to be racially alert must recognise as undeniable forecasts. For example, Alan Fenton, a social worker, walked into a dimly lit black hang-out, off the Westbourne Park Road in West London. Instantly, about 30 pairs of eyes followed him – Britain's lone white pioneer. 'Waddyah want?' shouted someone aggressively. 'To have a drink.' Three blacks moved up to him. 'Sorry boy,' said one, 'members only.' They had his arms, steering him towards the door.

'How do I get membership?' Fenton asked hurriedly. 'When you join.' The door flicked open. They let him go. He turned slowly (here, that's how a white has to move) to a blockade of hate. 'Who do I apply to?' Expectations in the room were high. 'You can't.' And not realising he was addressing an audience very touchy about put-downs, 'Well, how can I join when I can't apply?' He thought he had them. 'That's your problem, man.' He was forced out.

Amazingly, seconds later, he reappeared with two friends. 'Look,' he began, 'let's be reasonable . . .' He was cut off. Liberal reason is a commodity in short supply. Immediately, four other blacks joined the original three. Two with knives, one armed with a possession now common amongst some black militants – a small pistol. 'The talk is over.' With that, Fenton was kneed in the balls, falling out . . . It was over in seconds. His friends hadn't moved since they entered. They left, backing out. This is, without a doubt, a no go area for whites. Here, if your colour's not in – you're out.

Among young blacks and Asians there is a growing number whose attitude towards the whites is not hardening, but has already hardened. After the recent slaying of a youth in Southall, Asians, often considered to be passive, changed. Today, vigilante groups operate in a well-organised grapevine in many Asian communities. Now they retaliate if provoked. For instance, six weeks ago, a defence force was created in Brick Lane E1 because of persistent aggro from the National Front.

In Brixton, the artery of the black community, pioneer streets have fallen into even more squalor. As unemployment increases, slums spread. And grievances fester. Here, below the slowly cohering top layer of blacks (traders in Brixton market), poor blacks wait, sporadically employed and disgruntled. They pass the time on street corners, talking, drinking, smoking and listening to countless funky records. Day in, day out. Their discontent growing in the sunshine and storm of racial politics. Their attitude to whites not hardening – but hardened. In parts, certainly along Railton Road SE24, the atmosphere is permeated by simmering tensions.

Anything can, and does, happen. Some of this tension expressed itself in a fight I saw between blacks when a scuffle broke out over a spilled drink. Two protagonists emerged, one with an iron pipe, the other with an empty Coke bottle. The pipe shattered the bottle. The jagged neck remained. It happened fast, against a background of shouting and jeering. They are pulled apart. An old Jamaican at my table said these youths have 'studied different'. 'They're as disunited as we are, but more definitely against whites . . .' continuing, 'very few of them would go with a white' and, significantly, '. . . that counts for their unity. . .' A unity against whites.

The quarter mile between Desmond's Hip City record shop and

Mecca Bookmakers has seen and continues to see, bitter conflicts between police and blacks. It is not surprising that this section is now known locally as 'the front line'. The activity denoted by that name speaks for itself. Now that firearms are obtainable by some black militants (who are admittedly a minority at present), the ingredients of big trouble are here. I've seen it. I'm black. If I'd been white, I might not have done so.

But white Britain has consistently persuaded itself that black and Asian people will permanently put up with their oppression. In a society subscribing to the Utopian ideal of freedom of speech (which suggests freedom of thought), black criticism is tolerated as long as there is no action. And what of black and Asian warnings of dire consequences, like, 'it could happen here'? 'Poppycock, that coon was probably writing with his foot,' or 'I do think you're being a little over-sensitive.' The dismissive tactics come into play: people see it, they rationalize it, they walk away from it and then refute it. Was it ever written or said at all?

In March, 1980, in St Paul's, Bristol, the unrealistic statement 'It couldn't happen here' was shattered. The disturbances were due to an oppressive white society which had decided that its short-term vision of life was truth, for everybody. But through a white-accepted participation of racism in the warped British practice of democracy, a sophisticated form of *apartheid* has developed, promoting the leading question, what is life like for blacks and Asians living in Britain today? In October 1976, in the *New Statesman* I wrote an article under the title, 'Dagenham's Way with Colour'. The article stated:

Henry Ford, founder of the Ford empire and innovator of mass production, has always been considered a man ahead of his time. Certainly his dictum about the original Model T – 'You can have any colour you want, so long as it's black' – seems to apply equally well today at Ford's Dagenham Estate. Except an onlooker there might easily think he had meant, in fact, people and not cars.

Of Dagenham's 23,000 workers, 60 per cent are black or Asian. In the body plant, 70 per cent of 6,000 workers are black or Asian, and in the PTA (Paint, Trim and Assembly) section the figure is 60 per cent of 5,000. However, of 1,200 foremen, only six are black and the figures for shop stewards are barely more impressive: ten out of 300. These numbers speak for themselves; blacks form the majority of the workforce, but they are thinly represented when it comes to trade union or staff appointments. According to Sid Harraway, boss of the shop stewards' committee: 'You'd be right in thinking that the ratio is all wrong.' Ford-worker Herman Pinnock commented: 'We have very few of everything black, except non-skilled production workers.'

With varying degrees of justification, black and Asian workers believe management to be racially prejudiced. It has been assumed that trade unions were not. Yet, most remarkably, Dagenham has never seen the promotion of a black man from shop steward to convener or district official level. Is it lace-curtain discrimination that inhibits blacks from attempting to climb the ladder? If so, is the discrimination at management level, or is it within the unions themselves? Or a combination of both? According to one black worker: 'Some of us have applied many times, but without success. Now many have developed a segregation mentality.'

The existence of veiled discrimination might go some way towards explaining why Bill Morris is the only black full-time official of the TGWU. And possibly it could explain, too, why Britain's largest union, with 1.7 million members (of whom 287,000 are women), has only one female official at the national level. She is Marie Patterson, and despite her token-female loneliness, Ron Todd, secretary of TGWU's Region 1, maintains: 'It is not a male preserve. Other than Ms Patterson, a woman has not yet emerged as the best person.' His stand on the other question is as adamant. He maintains that no racism exists in his organisation, and if he discovered a racist shop steward he would dump him 'because I don't think it's compatible with being a union representative'.

But there is still the curious lack of black stewards and officials, and Mr Todd could not deny that the few there are hardly make for a racially integrated union movement. According, however, to a Ford official 'they don't have what it takes'. What does 'it' take? After a week at Dagenham you really begin to understand the cynicism of automobile workers, but the magical 'it' never becomes apparent. New workers are given a talk by a shop steward, and also by safety and personnel officers. Then, training: 'A *great* training programme,' as one of them said, 'two days, I think. You don't have to be full of "O" levels to work here.' Once trained, it's on the line. 'Hello,' says Bill. 'You put this here, so. And put that there, got it?' Then, mysteriously, as if it were all in the nature of a favour: 'I'm not paid for this, y'know.' A new worker either picks up the routine, or picks up his cards.

Real arguments or racial resentments are not aired on the factory floor. 'These fights,' one worker says, 'happen outside the gates or in the pubs. But the tension is there most of the time.' 'The whole history of endeavouring to prove discrimination,' says Sid Harraway, 'is very difficult.' One Ford worker who might agree with this is Olatunji Taylor who, in 1971, applied for the post of trainee foreman. 'At the present time there are no vacancies,' he was told by the personnel officer, Mr Rossiter. But 'your application will receive consideration'.

Between 1971 and 1973 Taylor applied several more times with no tangible results, except that he was advised to re-apply in 1976. Feeling he was being discriminated against, Mr Taylor took his case to the Race Relations Board. Thirteen months, 16 letters, and four changes of Board Officials later he was told that 'no unlawful discrimination had taken place'. (My own enquiries at the Race Relations Board produced the reply: 'We are not allowed to discuss any case which has not already received publicity.' A nice little catch-22 phrase, but small comfort to Mr Taylor.)

Doggedly, Taylor applied yet again in May 1976. In an interview with Mr Rossiter he was told that he was an unsuitable candidate because he hadn't the personality required, nor the ability to lead. Curiously, though, Rossiter suggested he apply again in 12 months. He was, in the meantime, to 'reassess yourself and your attitudes'. When asked to enlarge on this somewhat arcane advice Mr Rossiter told me over the phone that he did not wish to make any comment at this stage. Nonetheless, he did so. Taylor, he said, 'fell down in various respects' and 'does not meet the requirements'. It was stressed that Taylor could always apply again. This is all very well, but 45 is the age limit for foreman training, and as

Taylor is now 41 he does not have many chances left.

What has Mr Taylor's union done about his case? Shop steward Alex French, who had initially helped Mr Taylor, was told by Ford's that 'the union was not allowed to be party to any discussions on the appointment of foreman; it is a management function only'. This is apparently true, and it may be here that the union has surrendered some of its power to protect its members' rights. There is, of course, a recognised grievance procedure which can be invoked in cases of racial discrimination within a union. However, the process for registering and following through a complaint is very complex and would require a high degree of patience, courage and persistence for any grievance to be remedied. Among black and Asian workers, already handicapped by language and sophistication barriers, there exists, too, a fear of losing their jobs if they become known as trouble-makers. For these reasons, complaints such as Mr Taylor's tend not to filter up to union leaders, who, therefore, continue blithely to assume there is little trouble of a racial nature among their members.

According to a PEP survey, racial problems in the trade unions fall into two groups. In the first, the local union tolerates discrimination rather than acting to counter it. In the second, the union is not directly involved in discriminatory practices but such practices have, nonetheless, been allowed to develop. It is possible that Olatunji Taylor's case falls within this second group. Either way black workers are the casualties.

David Buckle, district officer of the TGWU based at British Leyland's Cowley plant, feels the most dangerous thing is for those in the trades union movement to 'kid ourselves that there is *not* discrimination in our unions'. Most significantly he says: 'What is going on in our society is going on in the trade union movement. It simply reflects the kind of society we've got.' The reflection is unfortunately, an unflattering one. If Olatunji Taylor's case is representative of black workers there is a very real risk that, discouraged by the failure of their attempts to gain promotion, they will become another unleavened lump of discontent in British industry.

How long before Britain sees and has to suffer a black workers' reaction to their second-rate position? It is on the cards, for the longest road has an end.

Today, in white immigrant-minded Britain, racism is impregnated powerfully into the white struggle against black and Asian human rights, and into the mind of the black and Asian body politic; through a successive series of undermining immigration controls, thus keeping the black and Asian whipping-boys 'mobile-minded': 'We don't want you coons to settle, you might think it's permanent – this is *not* your country.' A Britannic Reversal. Maybe the sun never really set on the British Empire, because God does not trust the Brits in the dark. Who does?

In Britain, racism is a highly inflammable issue, which is the foundation of her system of justice, her criminal law and the current white prejudices and negative attitudes toward black and Asian people. Immigration, quickly followed by other issues, was the first fundamental white assault on the black and Asian community. Immigration also prevented political unification of the so-called immigrants by diverting their attentions; and the immigrating statutory instruments surrounding the blacks and Asians, designed specifically for *them* by government of both political colours, completed the white immigration gang warfare.

In *Now You Do Know*, author John Downing, writing about immigration, stated:

When the 1971 Act cancelled the previous right of black Commonwealth members to citizenship after five years' residence in Britain, it created a situation where any black person walking the streets might be a post-1971 Act entrant. White immigrants did not stand out as much; black people wore no tag or lapel-button to indicate the date of their entry to Britain. Since the Act also gave the police the right to stop and search people in the street, or break into private premises without a warrant, if they had 'reasonable grounds' to suspect the presence of illegal immigrants, the police had carte blanche to harass black people on this pretext . . .

At airports as well, black people are regularly subjected to vaginal or anal examinations by immigration officials under pretext of a search for drugs, or checking for diseases, or at one time – until protests cancelled this excuse – to satisfy the officer that the woman was a virgin. It must be stressed that this loathsome behaviour, though congruent with the National Front and Powellite sympathies of many immigration officials, is perfectly legal under the 1971 Act.

Other practices include abusive questioning, separating parents and children and grilling them separately on details of their application form for entry; and a readiness to interpret the slightest such deviation, or the most marginal indication of a willingness to work during a holiday trip, as evidence of duplicity, and therefore a reason to refuse admission. In their time, British immigration officials have preferred to shuttle destitute British citizens of Asian descent around the world's airlines for weeks at a time rather than let them in.

Those who have been refused entry but who succeed in registering a rapid appeal against refusal, are kept in special detention centres, Harmondsworth near Heathrow airport being the best known. Conditions in these centres are pointlessly harsh, with inmates not allowed to rest on their beds during the day, with great difficulty of access for relatives, with inappropriate food, one telephone, and an extremely unpleasant attitude on the part of the Securicor guards. (The use of private police for public purposes is a dimension of contemporary policing not covered in II.d; that it should begin with black people is typical of the process.) The objective is clear: to grind in the message that black people are not wanted in Britain (Moore and Wallace 1975). The message is intended to spread out from those treated in this way, to as wide an audience as possible, nationally and internationally. State policy and immigration officials' attitudes are at one with each other. This hostile treatment arises because those who apply for immigration control work are given the necessary scope by the immigration rules to act out their prejudices.

In times like these, of social crisis springing from the racial hailstorm beating down on black and Asian skulls, it is easy to be hoodwinked by the strength and depth of white racist attacks, and by the white mania for tribal security. It is easy to mistake eventful time-bound occurrences for never-ending reality. But the potency and unchangeability of the white kick-back is deceptive. Although this offensive engagement appears to have unflagging power, the necessary political ideas, however, are very much in the hands of those whites who have unfettered themselves from the myopia of Empire mentality, and those whites, blacks and Asians who have unshackled themselves from the lord/serf mentality.

However, there are other unhealthy stirrings on the national front. 'A great philosophy', said Charles Péguy, 'is not one that passes final judgements and establishes ultimate truth. It is one that causes uneasiness and starts commotion.' Péguy has a point, and the 'uneasiness and commotion' he speaks of, in this instance, is the British Nationality Bill 1981. It is a bill which suggests that Britain entered the race conflict by accident and now intends to exit by design. This political instrument, supposedly intended to streamline the rules and regulations about what constitutes a British citizen, is seen by its proponents as the white man's oasis in a racial desert of despair. In February 1981, *The Sunday Times* wrote:

> The new law will introduce three tiers of citizenship – British citizenship, British overseas citizenship, and citizenship of the British dependent territories. Only the first of these confers the normal full citizenship rights. Being born in Britain will no longer be enough to claim full citizenship on. Babies born abroad to parents themselves born abroad, even if they are British will not automatically be deemed fully British.
>
> The final decision rests on the Home Office 'discretion' and this could apply to millions of cases. Passport offices will demand evidence about parents' birth as well as the applicants'. The new law will also tangle inextricably with the various Immigration Acts (1962, 1968 and 1971).
>
> Both the Labour and Liberal parties have declared the Bill to be racist and it is expected to take a long time going through the committee stage.

A briefing published by the Action Group on Immigration and Nationality in October 1980 stated:

> It is never easy for a country to re-define its nationality, but it has often been done. Problems little different from, or harder than, ours have been dealt with by nations which used to have larger overseas empires, such as France, Portugal and the Netherlands. France, for example, has a single nationality which carries the same rights for all holders and is held by people in the Overseas Departments (Martinique, Guadeloupe, Réunion) equally with people in metropolitan France. French citizens in all these territories can move freely in and out of them all: a black French citizen from Martinique can enter France freely and work there; a white French citizen can enter and work in Martinique; both can vote for the French Assembly and both have freedom-of-movement rights in the EEC. But former French possessions which have become independent countries have completely separate nationalities of their own, with no citizens' rights in France (e.g. Algeria, Chad).
>
> The other colonial powers used to have different classes of citizenship, with different rights from each other, but since 1945 they have moved towards defining a single, clear nationality. The United Kingdom is going in exactly the opposite direction: it used to have one category for the whole Empire, but is now moving towards a ranking of superior and inferior classes, as though legislating for an empire that is now only a ghost.

It's that Empire mentality again. The international uproar over the white immigrants in South Africa and their system of 'separate development' known as apartheid, stems from the fact that racism is written into their constitution, along with their capitalistic need for black enslavement. In Britain racism has not needed to be written into British law. Subtlety has hitherto been used as the racists' weapon. A racist Nationality Act implies that that subtlety has failed, blacks, Asians and some whites having seen through it, and a majority of whites now demand open hostility to blacks and Asians.

Considering that the white Establishment minority fears a white working-class mass rejection of their conditioned docility, a Declaration of Human Rights must be avoided at all costs for the sake of keeping alive the status quo. Therefore, it should come as no surprise that the United Kingdom now wishes to declare what blacks, Asians and a white minority have known all along, that she intends to 'come out' by openly clasping to her superior bosom the doctrine of separate development by separately developing a first-class nationality for whites and a second-class one for blacks and Asians. So where to? Soweto? So, finally, we have the truth. Her Majesty's Government intends to stitch racism onto Britain's Constitutional blanket. The world, my friends, is definitely changing, for Doctor Footswitch is here. But, will Britain's vociferous anti-apartheid movement have the courage and the commonsense to demonstrate against British as it has continued to do against Britain's disaster-prone cousins in South Africa?

In a *Guardian* article of July 1980, Mrs Anne Dummett of the Joint Council for the Welfare of Immigrants was quoted as stating:

People should realise that the new category of British citizen with its rights of entry and abode in Britain, would be largely white, and the category of British overseas citizen, with no rights to anything, would be largely black.

So, let us make no mistake, the British Nationality Act today will be the gun in the hands of its victims, tomorrow. 'Some people are moulded by their admirations, others by their hostilities' (Elizabeth Bowen, *The Death of the Heart*).

To a swelling *guilt-fermenting* catalogue of expressions which intensifies the British educational Establishment's class-conscious sufferings, tack on the terms 'racist' and 'racism'. In the *Times Educational Supplement* of June 1981, journalist Diane Spencer wrote:

Mr Donald Frith, general secretary of the Secondary Heads Association thought it 'scandalous to use the word "racist" as if it had a precise meaning, I find its use bitterly unhelpful – it is a term of abuse.'

There is in this statement the institutionalized 'deny-it-first' British habit, which comes into play whenever the uncomfortable cries of 'racism' (or sexism) rear their heads. Through this statement we can detect the paramount white need to deny flatly black accusational opinion, without consideration. And seen against the backdrop of current racial tensions in all areas of Britain's social life, this revocation of the existence of racial antagonism in British schools is tantamount to implying: 'I cannot come to terms with unpleasant realities, so let us sweep it under the carpet by repudiating its existence; that way it might miraculously vanish.' The Head-in-the-sand syndrome. The glaring facts are that, inside Britain's Houses of Knowledge, white teachers have given little quality time to those pupils who are, by white custom, not to be mentioned together with anything positive. Those pupils I refer to are The Unmentionables, the blacks. It is true that racism and education should be completely unfamiliar to one another. But in Britain, if you are black or Asian, racism *is* education; in fact, i.e. through the constant teaching of negatives about black and Asian people found in Britain's history books; and in fiction, e.g. the perpetuation, by white teachers, of the fallacies and myths about blacks being good at sport and music. Therefore, black pupils are encouraged at sport and not at academic subjects. There is a profound inability within the school system to promote and encourage black pupils to stay on and achieve. At this point the fundamental question must be: inside a racist atmosphere do people lose their prejudiced feelings on becoming teachers? Especially after their own conditioned schoolings about black and Asian people, when they were pupils themselves. In the Inner London Education Authorities' house newspaper, *Contact*, the issue of June 1981, observing the Interim Report of the Committee of Inquiry into the Education of Children from Minority Ethnic Groups (Rampton Committee), it stated:

> Although the Committee believes that only a small number of teachers could be said to be racist in the commonly accepted

sense, it believes that other teachers display signs of '*unintentional*' racism which may influence their attitude towards ethnic minority pupils. [My italics]

Bernard Coard, author of *How the West Indian Child is Made Educationally Sub-Normal in the British School System* published by New Beacon Books, pointed out a virulent aspect of the Rampton Committee's definition of 'unintentional'. He stated:

An Inner London Education Authority report entitled *The Education of Immigrant Pupils in Special Schools for Educationally Subnormal Children* (ILEA 657) reveals that five of their secondary ESN schools had more than 30 per cent immigrant pupils at the time of their survey in 1967. By January 1968, one of the schools had 60 per cent immigrant children!

In the ILEA's ESN (Special) Day Schools, over 28 per cent of all the pupils are immigrant, *compared with only 15 per cent immigrants in the ordinary schools* of the ILEA. This situation is particularly bad for the West Indians, because three-quarters of all the immigrant children in these Educationally Subnormal schools are West Indian, whereas *West Indians are only half of the immigrant population in the ordinary schools*. The 1970 figures are even more alarming, for even though immigrants comprise nearly 17 per cent of the normal school population nearly 34 per cent of the ESN school population is immigrant. And four out of every five immigrant children in these ESN schools are West Indian!

The ILEA report quoted by Bernard Coard also gave the numbers of black children attending ESN schools whom the headmasters of those schools thought were wrongly placed: one school calculated that between seventy and seventy-nine per cent of its black children were wrongly placed; two schools calculated that between forty and forty-nine per cent of black children were wrongly placed; another considered that between thirty and thirty-nine per cent were wrongly placed; and three schools calculated that between twenty and twenty-nine per cent of their black children were wrongly placed.

Bernard Coard added:

> . . . nine out of nineteen schools thought that 20 per cent or more of their immigrant pupils had been wrongly placed. This is from Table 9, page 9, of the report. The report states (page 5) that: 'Where children are suspected as being wrongly placed in the ESN school, this is *four times as likely* in the case of immigrant pupils.' [Author's italics]

Due to the unexpected gutbuckets of wrath poured out by black parents against the excessive loading of black children into those schools, the educational Establishment, which by now saw them as lands of darkness by virtue of how many black children they had exiled to them, mugged by their undisguised disinterest in black education, suffered withdrawal symptoms. And 'procrastination being the art of keeping up with yesterday' (Don Marquis), the educational Establishment certainly has done so. Keep on keeping on, with the art of sham. This ESN black-loading sham has re-emerged as the Disruptive Pupils Programme (ILEA 1979), which in secondary schools has resulted in Sanctuaries and Off-Site Support Centres. In primary schools they are aptly entitled Peripatetic Groups, Nurture Groups and Withdrawal Groups. Very magniloquent titles, but what do they mean? They, successors of ESN schools, revamped in name only, *are* ESN schools. The possibility of any of their black pupils being re-admitted to normal schooling is practically non-existent; and white children are prominent by their absence from these units.

Peter Wilby, *The Sunday Times* Education Correspondent, wrote in May 1980 that the existence of these 'sinbins' is a cause for concern. He stated:

> A new survey by the Advisory Centre for Education shows that local education authorities have set up at least 450 sinbins – double the number in operation three years ago.
>
> ACE calls them 'a threat to the rights of parents and schoolchildren' and, with the National Association for Multi-racial Education, is holding a conference next week to highlight the problem. It will be told that:

– sinbin children are rarely returned to normal schooling;
– there is a disproportionate number of black children involved;
– the children often end up with a second-class education in sub-standard conditions.

. . . ACE says the procedures for sending children to them are too varied and too vague. In at least one area, the children may be attending the unit because they are 'peevish, dreamy, unpersevering, depressed and untidy' as well as because they are 'bullying and destructive.'

If a child is expelled, or sent to a school for the sub-normal or maladjusted, the authorities must go through formalities and give parents rights of appeal. Sinbins, by contrast, have no legal status and a child can be sent to one – without the parents having any say.

But the parents of those children had dreams. And they worked. What black parents endured so that they might give their children the opportunity of education cannot be quantified; nor can the humiliations those parents had to suffer when their children returned home from ESN schools more un-educated than before they left. I can see the pain, the sweat and the tears. I can also hear the white man's denials.

The Rampton Committee, with its now famed Rampton Report, comforted those parents with a new set of figures. Their report showed that three per cent of West Indian school leavers gain five O-levels. Ironically, the Rampton Committee had unknowingly provided a yardstick which can be used to measure the level of racism crushing the young blacks attending English schools; a level which now, using 1981 Rampton figures, suggests that black children have to withstand a high level of racism while attending English schools. Well done, Britannia.

Or is their failure rate due to the perpetuated white myth that black people possess a lower IQ than whites? If that is true, metaphorically speaking, then Britain's multi-racial society will never see a black man or woman rise to any level higher than the ground floor. Which also might suggest that, due to black repugnance at the positively-motivating-to-fail white IQ test, and visualizing the possibility (through the black genetic instincts of slavery-avoidance) that they may never ascend, or afford that luxury known as 'aspiring', they may choose to take up other methods to attain their just education rights.

The Rampton Committee also provided another set of figures, regarding Asians. Eighteen per cent of Asian school leavers gained five O-levels. Could this be due to the fact that white Britain never fractionalized Asian societies, like they did the black? The Asian family unit is still culturally intact; thus affording some Asian school children a steadier home life in which to study. Whereas the whites uprooted black people from their cultural roots through the slave trade and maintained the separation of African blacks from Africa so that the enforced emigrants could never regain their rightful hereditary links. Those blacks were murdered physically, spiritually and morally through the destruction of the black family unit in the West Indies. That there is still today a black family unit in the West Indies at all, only goes to demonstrate the strength and determination of the black people who were forced to reside there.

Of course black parents have a responsibility to help education authorities with the educating of their children. Furthermore the re-built black family unit in Britain has recovered sufficiently from white repression to be strong enough to help and care for the education of their children. But do whites want to recognize that fact? Are teachers aware enough?

Which leads us on to the next divisive white tactic. A tactic perfected in Britain's ex-colonies in Africa and the West Indies. The Asian Buffer Syndrome. In those colonies, Indians were transported by Britain's whites to act as buffers between the black majority and a white-ruling minority. By placing Asians over Africa's blacks to act as foremen and junior managers, rewarding them by enabling them to set up as small businessmen, they, now a British-class above the blacks, made black armed insurrection more difficult. They acted as informers in order to keep the position they had attained, even though the mass of Asians in the then British Asia were just as oppressed as the black people living in British Africa. A false enmity grew, not just between the black people of Africa and those few Asians in Africa, but between the black and Asian nations, in general. The African result can be seen in this white-created problem which has left a very sad and difficult racial situation in Africa today, i.e. the Ugandan and Kenyan Asians. A tactic used successfully once, is one to be used again. Divide and rule.

The Rampton figures created the image that Asians are more intelligent than blacks, and therefore a class above them. The British media used it, and the white population had grown used to hearing it, while subconsciously believing it. But because black and Asian peoples have seen through that white divisive device, it has lost its potency and it will not work again.

Sadly, what the Rampton Committee's Report really underlines is that there is an overall failure in the education of Britain's white, brown and black schoolchildren which is what this nation should be very concerned about, instead of making opportunistic political use of black and brown people as scapegoats for national educational failure, and continuing to ignore the real and obvious implications of the Rampton Report.

Philosopher Bertrand Russell, in his book entitled *Power* published in 1938, honing his grey matter with moral reasoning, pointed to reality with 'this is where it's at':

> As the beliefs and habits which have upheld traditional power decay, it gradually gives way either to power based upon some new belief, or to 'naked' power, i.e. to the kind that involves no acquiescence on the part of the subject. Such is the power of the butcher over the sheep, of an invading army over a vanquished nation, and of the police over detected conspirators. The power of the Catholic Church over Catholics is tradition, but its power over heretics who are persecuted is naked. The power of the State over loyal citizens is traditional, but its *power over rebels is naked*. Organisations that have a long career of power pass, as a rule, through three phases: first, that of fanatical but not traditional belief, leading to conquest; then, that of general acquiescence in the new power, which rapidly becomes traditional; and finally that in which power, being now used against those who reject tradition, has again become naked.
>
> [My italics]

Consequently, it is through those who do not conform that we can truly witness the naked power of the state and its institutions. The British education system is about conformity. Rightly or wrongly, therein lies Britain's stability. The majority, being a reliable army of conformists, have, by Bertrand Russell's definition, acquiesced.

Schools, therefore, severely curb the natural tendency of a child for individuality. They temper that instinct just sufficiently to conform that child to the will of the state; which twists its direction so that he or she becomes the factory-fodder of Britain's concrete jungles, or, the heir to its controls.

However, there exists in Britain a selection of non-conformists. Some through their beliefs, i.e. campaigners against injustices; Some through their political beliefs, i.e. Marxists; some by accident, i.e. the unemployed; some by misfortune, i.e. the handicapped; some through their sex, i.e. women; and others are seen as non-conformists through the nature of their non-conformity, which is their black and brown pigmentation. A fact which obviously permeated through to the classroom, by being an inherent part of a racialistic society.

More solidly, do the racial leanings of Britain's white teaching-majority guide the practices of their teachings, by teaching white?

White is right, and black gets the sack. ESN forever. So, what is *contemporary* education for? And what are Britain's schools today educating toward? Divide and rule, as ever?

Most nightmares end at daybreak; Britain's, in education, is just beginning.

5

The Order Architects

The British police force is the wince of the nerve of the capitalist's frown and the organ of coercion for the State. This national all-weather bag-of-tricks is a social knuckle-duster in the battleground of rebel deterrence; thus enabling the rule of law, through the shrapnel of the Blue Eminence, to prevail. That *is* the Standing Order. Created by the state to guarantee public obedience on behalf of the ruling propertied minority, which is seen to be in the so-called interests of the majority, these order-architects are paid legal informers. And On Her Majesty's Service, the policeman is your statutory friend. He can also be your Judas, so as to curb the natural tendencies of the non-conforming; who, in his eyes, are permanently a hair's breadth removed from criminality. Thus he is ordained by the state to use his own discretion, when the rule of law has been infringed, in the amount of naked power needed as a remedy.

Power is a magnet for the self-revering and it demands a degree of megalomania from those who *seek* it. Bertrand Russell, in his philosophy of power, in his book entitled *Power,* wrote:

> Thus love of power, as a motive, is limited by timidity, which also limits the desire for self-direction. Since power enables us

to realize more of our desires than would otherwise be possible, and since it secures deference from others, it is natural to desire power except in so far as timidity interferes. This sort of timidity is lessened by the habit of responsibility, and accordingly responsibilities tend to increase the desire for power. Experience of cruelty and unfriendliness may operate in either direction: with those who are easily frightened it produces the wish to escape observation, while bolder spirits are stimulated to seek positions in which they can inflict cruelties rather than suffer them.

Consequently, it is inherent in the act of joining a police force that an individual, consciously or subconsciously, seeks a larger slice of the local power-cake. And it is in the position of being a police officer, that an individual in civil life comes closest to the smell of individual power of the naked kind. But, as guardians of the law they are morally assumed to be above misusing it. Obviously, effective policing through a willing public co-operation ensures that the use of his naked power is rarely needed. Conformity, being the secret police of the majority's senses, aids the policeman in the everyday execution of his duties. Therefore, non-conformers are seen, by the police, to be in direct need of external and visible policing.

But it will be a defunct nation which possesses no police force, and conversely, a nation with a police force allowed to misuse its invested power can hold that nation or an element of that nation in sheer terror; such is the power a nation invests in its police force.

Policemen are an integral part of this class-ridden society. They uphold the law through the ambitious white Darwinian maxim 'survival of the fittest'. The fittest in the public eye are the propertied, and the rule of law is all about protecting property. In the Higher Mathematics of the police 'the fittest' are the best, the upper and middle classes. But, it is 'tough luck' for the masses, who co-operate easily, through their greater numbers and lack of influence, with the promotional prospects of that officer. Being fair game, the chances of the white working-classes depend upon the nature of the individual lonely God of the street, in blue, and the mood he is in on that particular day. Have you ever witnessed the sycophantic crawlings of a policeman in the presence of a peer of the realm or an industrialist?

Additionally, a police officer who recognizes that a citizen is without power, through lack of influence or social status, has it made. That citizen, by virtue of his negative-power situation, normally submits, especially if the officer is of the tyrannical kind. But in doing so he might have to admit guilt so as to soften the action of this tyrant. In raw reality, everything else being pretence, a citizen with no social standing or connections, in the hands of this policing state functionary, is already in a hopeless position, being unrecognized for his social value. Anything is allowed, and does happen, to citizens like himself.

Such are the benefits of an enterprising class system, and such are the benefits of enterprise. Tom Bowden, author of *Beyond the Limits of the Law*, states:

> For the poor, the dispossessed and the underprivileged, for those without property and hence with no stake in the system, the police appear more often as aloof and brutal authoritarians . . .
>
> . . .We have said that the evidence supports the view that the policeman is a conventional personality; that he is politically and morally conservative and operates in such an environment that all his values and beliefs are based on the fact that he is *for* order and *against* change. In normal times, but particularly in crises, the policeman works to uphold or restore the *status quo*.

Therefore, through its worship of the god of property, and especially of those to whom it belongs, the British police force is itself the personalized property of those who have it, the British ruling class.

The reality of this was reported in *The Sunday Times* of July 1981:

> An inquiry has been ordered by Scotland Yard into last week's death of a mentally disturbed man who lost consciousness in a struggle with police summoned to take him to hospital.
>
> The investigation will try to find out how nine policemen

came to overpower 27-year-old Winston Rose, a West Indian from Leyton, East London, who had a history of mental illness but who, according to his wife, had never been violent. It will also examine certain allegations that Rose was thrown facedown into a police van after losing consciousness . . .

. . . 'Two policemen tried to hold him. Then there were about eight policemen on top of him. I couldn't see him for policemen. One of them said: "Use your radio." What he meant I don't know. One of them said, "He's pretending to go unconscious." I saw a hand on a truncheon, I don't know if he was getting it out or putting it away.' . . .

. . . 'The police carried him out and threw him into the van. One of them said, "Face downwards," and they turned him over. They just threw him in like a piece of meat.'

The blue-rinse pretence of flexibility of Britain's police forces has always been and is still a useful psychological image-softening weapon by presuming the gullibility of the British public into believing that advertised police image. But since there is a latent mania for power lying in cold storage inside every police individual, the Toytown Noddy-image of the smiling 'unarmed bobby' you could talk to, ask the advice of and more unrealistically, trust, is fake. There is a massive difference between this advertised image and the cosh on the head of Blair Peach.

However, *the police are tragically powerless if they are not supported by public sentiment and that public sentiment is powerful when supported by the police.* Therefore police will react to any national crisis, psychologically and then physically. The police being part of the white national-mind are themselves subject to any mass paranoia sweeping the country at any given moment. In their position of being the guardians of the law they are selective when using their naked power in reaction to mass fear and mass ignorance. Like it or not, contemporary police behaviour is a reflection of the type of society we live in; a society ruled by the mass white-subscription to the ethic of white superiority. The difference between the police and the public is that the white public individual possesses an indirect power (i.e. the vote) which he cannot *legally* use directly on those whom he dislikes or fears.

But the policeman vested with naked power for use against those whom the state views as non-conformist, (e.g. rebels or, as we have seen, the mentally handicapped, or those who intend to disrupt the workings of the state) can also secretly, in Britain's case not so secretly, oppress those he *knows* will produce very little outcry from the majority of the public who are white. Black and Asian people just happen to fit very neatly into this category. The problem here is that since there is white mass hysteria about the presence of black and Asian people in Britain, in the eyes of the police those black and brown individuals are fair game since injustice only really exists in the eyes of the white power structure, where one of their own race had his or her rights denied. But there are exceptions to the rulers' rule. Once there is a *majority* dislike of a person or community, that individual or community, from that moment on loses all their human rights, for example the Jeremy Thorpe public and media crucifixion. But the white working classes, too busy with conforming or rebelling (thus defending themselves), have little interest in defending the rights of those they themselves are frightened of. Black and Asian people are therefore abandoned to the tender mercies of the blue hot-shots in their houses of pain, if they happen to suffer the misfortune of stumbling across the statutory muscles of the law. Tough luck for the restless natives.

I wonder if the British system's racial ethics, of denying rights to blacks and Asians, coincides with Articles 1 and 2 of the Universal Declaration of Human Rights (1948), which states:

Article 1
All human beings are born free and equal in dignity and rights.
Article 2
Everyone is entitled to all the rights and freedoms set forth in this Declaration, without distinction of any kind, such as race, colour, sex, language, religion, political or other opinion, national or social origin, property, birth or other status.

Or does Britain's system only pay lip-service to those articles, considering itself above them? In that case do you recognize *anything* British about the following statement published in 1967 by UNESCO in a book entitled *Apartheid*, about black people in another white-dominated society (albeit a white minority), in South Africa? It states:

> Thus, unless teachers are aware that nearly all textbooks perpetuate errors which historians have corrected by diligent research . . . children in many schools will regard the Xhosa as thieves and possibly murderers, and the European farmers as blameless, since many of the books employ . . . emotive words calculated to arouse feelings of hostility against the Xhosa. The children are therefore likely to identify themselves virtuously with the blameless farmers, and some, if not all, present-day Africans with the Xhosa thieves.

Ironically, hitherto in Britain, major problems have decisively evolved an answer, or an individual to 'answer the call', e.g. Winston Churchill for World War Two. All, that is, except this one, of *race*. Britain has never been so faced with what her whites obviously consider to be the 'enemy within'. Therefore, because of the urgent requirement for a solution to this white-created crisis, the question that begs itself is: 'Is there a giant conspiracy by Britain's whites against her blacks and Asians?' No. It is a conditioned way of life for many, but not all, of Britain's whites. But, sadly, it is also an attitude which exists deeply embedded in large quantities in much of this nation's police forces; who now find themselves in the 'inquisitor's dilemma'; kissed-to-life by the hair-raising methods they have used on blacks and Asians in places such as Brixton. Some of these police procedures have even made the national flesh creep. For instance, Britain's white community was shocked by the 1.55 a.m. police raid on some residents living in Railton Road, Brixton, on 15 July 1981, when detectives allegedly stormtrooped the homes of blacks brandishing 'sledgehammers, pickaxe handles, pickaxes and crowbars' and smashed up their homes. Even the government, normally deaf to black cries of injustice, could not *afford* to ignore this blatant act of vandalism; especially after Lord 'Brixton' Scarman had visited these homes of devastation, and significantly 'commented' in the *Sunday Telegraph*, in July 1981:

> ... [an] inquiry [was] ordered by Mr Whitelaw, the Home Secretary, into a police raid last week in Brixton when detectives were accused of 'smashing up' houses owned by *coloured* people. [My italics. Which colour? White?]

Consequently, Brixton's all-night-soul-patrol, the recognized by all colours, lawful *peacekeeping* agents of the government, relentlessly inspecting black meat, are surprisingly stunned by the incredible results of their hit-and-run grapes of racial wrath from their permanent and persistent SWAMP squad.

The traditional outcome of such repeated repression, the result of which we have witness, internationally, which 'could never happen here', *has* happened here. And the party is over. That repression has created, and is still creating, black and Asian rebels against a society which still smugly *presumes* their allegiance while bowling their considered 'woolly' heads against a national test-bat of racial resentment or hate.

A person who is that victimized is tutored by necessity into the taking of the law into his own hands. He has no problems. But this society does; by not taking crucial notice that that possibility exists. In Britain, if this individual is black or Asian, he will fall into one of two categories: either he has a 'chip on his shoulder' and stands an odds-on chance of being diagnosed a 'paranoid schizophrenic', to join the disproportionate number of blacks and Asians languishing in Britain's prisons and mental institutions, with a little help from Electro-Convulsive Therapy (ECT) and major tranquillizers; or, he will (as in most societies) be labelled a fanatic, after society considers the depth of the premeditation required to carry out what should be known as the 'victim's rebellion'. And I don't mean burglary or the like. Fanatic? That may very well be true; even though he may have arrived at his destructive way-out through his consistent and persistent attempts at conversing with an Ultra . . . Deaf . . . Ear.

Talkers need Listeners. Conversely, Listeners need Talkers. Unless, that is, one side considers that what the other side is saying is of no interest to themselves, having already (in fact, long ago) made up their minds.

If that is the case, then some of Britain's police divisions can decisively consider who they think is most likely to be fanatical by white postdated proxy. For example, in Brixton where police/black/brown relationships have 'broken down' (with a little *help* from their 'friends', and through *that* political pressure), black and white residents have been pushed terrifyingly close to the point of no return. Which accentuates that these police acts have failed them conclusively and publicly by their own design. Or was it an accident? Of white purpose? So then, who should be trusted to police the police? Why should the Police Complaints Board be the final arbiter of public complaints against the police? Do the police consider themselves to be a government which through its behaviour demands an opposition? So, what does the crisis in Brixton really signify? Will the Rule of the Cosh be the gasp in our lives?

The Police Complaints Board, a shrouded assembly, is currently surrounded by controversy. A ridiculous understatement; it is a board which has no public confidence in it. Remember Countryman? What does public confidence mean, and what happens when it is lost?

Surely statutory powers investing potentially naked power on a human being demand a statutory obligation on the part of the state? That of providing a solidity of checks and balances which, in turn, checks the balance of that particular person. So that it gives more than just a 'reasonable' amount of confidence to those whom that naked power will possibly be used upon. Anything less than that is a mugging, soul-sibling of deception. Let us mow the blue lawn of controversy. It is *not* for the public to disprove the integrity of the British police force. It *is* for the police to be constantly proving their own integrity to those whom they serve, the British public, regardless of sex, class or colour. In this way they could reassure them that, on the taking up of their invested succulent power, they *accept* the responsibility that goes with their *theoretically* honourable, action-man duties. That is, if they consider their moral responsibilities are in the interests of every one, including themselves and not just the political interests of the government. Police arrogance, implied by their instant and constant dismissals of any criticism, has served to push them farther away from those they say they are 'protecting the rights' of. For a police force freed from public and media criticism exists only in a police state. Or is this a police state, stating benevolence for international inspection?

It is often said that people cannot rise above the limitations of their own characters. Nations and their institutions, including their police forces, have no other choice. To some people living in Britain's community, possessing a polygon of hues and shades, the relationship between them and their police is akin to space, an unreality, and in human terms it is the hyphen between fact and fiction. Remember, this is a nation in which reality has left imagination standing. So, converse with Britain's blacks and Asians, but always with history in mind.

When the sword of Damocles finally fell at the beginning of Britain's trade in slaves, it rooted her to the spot with myths about blacks and the grandeur of herself; encapsulated today in the white fake-finger journalism, about blacks and Asians, making the reliability of British media reports about black and Asian people instantly so questionable, thus dismissable. And since a gasp is the difference between the truth and a lie, so is Britain's media.

Typical of this attitude is the regular fitting of pathetic black stereotypes inside a plethora of nescient publications which white Britons constantly tranquillize themselves with. An addiction of heroin-type proportions supports their wishful thoughts of what black people supposedly are and what they hope they are. Consider, for example, the *Daily Telegraph*, June 1981, reviewing the book *Sambo Sahib: the Story of Little Black Sambo and Helen Bannerman*. The reviewer wrote:

> It seems *extraordinary* that that harmless late-Victorian nursery favourite, 'The Story of Little Black Sambo,' should, in the last ten years have stirred up a 'racist' controversy. But so it is. It has been cast out from public libraries, *particularly in America,* removed from children's recommended reading lists and

banished from race-conscious Kindergartens.

If the author were alive today she would be both grieved and astonished, but fortunately she is not . . . [My italics]

It is clear from this so-called review, that this reviewer has based the critique on the wrong assumptions. What is really meant by the use of the word *extraordinary,* is that white people are shell-shocked by being told, by blacks, to change radically the nature of the racial chess game they have constantly played with the black identity for centuries. Furthermore, books like the 'Sambo' series, have been demolished, *particularly in American* libraries, for an obvious reason. For the price in lives of not changing the majority's racial ignorance was too high.

Contemporarily, Britain's black racial philosophy has sprung from criticism of white racial beliefs, through their seeking of logical reasons with which they then formulate logical (to themselves only) arguments to reinforce their own beliefs in the inferiority of others. A greasy attempt has been made in this review. Further still, if Helen Bannerman, the author of the 'Sambo' books, were alive today, and living in America, she would not just be 'grieved and astonished', she wouldn't *be*. *Black Slang*, a Dictionary of Afro American Talk (edited by Clarence Major), states the following: SAMBO any black American who accepts meekly his or her oppression; from *Little Black Sambo*, a story with stereotypes that serve the purpose of propaganda.

Take *The Sunday Times* in April 1981, with a profile of Leslie Allen the American tennis player:

This black woman has a sense of humour . . . The *simple truth* is that, were she not black, very few of the articles written about her in the past two months – including this one – would have appeared.

The 'simple truth' is that this reporter, with some honesty, admits that whites, including himself, have always ignored black achievement: attached is the implication that she is now successful because whites recognize her. And should he be surprised that a black woman has a sense of humour? This is yet another of the thoughtless but offensive remarks made about black people by many whites.

The *Daily Telegraph*, in an article of April 1980, highlights the negative white approach to blacks and Asians which is popularly used *en masse* by the British media. The article began:

> *Immigrant* dissatisfaction with the legal system will come into acrimonious focus on Tuesday when a leading *West Indian* barrister appears before a disciplinary tribunal of the Senate of the Inns of Court and the Bar on charges of professional misconduct and conduct unbecoming to a barrister.
>
> Mr Rudy Narayan, a *Guyana-born* barrister, faces charges relating to a letter . . . [My italics]

How about, 'Black dissatisfaction', and 'leading black barrister' and do we need to know where he was born?

Notice the imaginative use of the term 'immigrant'. But when is an immigrant not an immigrant? When he is white and has it covered by being a 'settler'. Also, notice that in Britain her whites continue to insist on the term immigrants for a people who came in peace by invitation.

When Britain's whites arrived to colonize Africa and Asia, with heavy immoral inspiration, they, on arrival, immediately labelled themselves 'settlers'. These houses of knowledge, hot-shots at everything and iced to other forms of human life, created an Auschwitz-type jam-session, by proceeding to settle their score through unsettling everything else. Their militaristic juke-box played songs of massacres of hundreds of thousands of blacks and browns. They butchered their families, raped their women, squandered the lives of their children. And finally, as their Act of Settlement, through fraudulent conversion, the light-fingered white settlers robbed the blacks and browns of their land. That is the white man's definition of settler, which stands as active today as it did when they originated their kleptomania of blacks and browns and their possessions.

This Mickey Mouse imaginative use of the word settler artfully conjures up a positive image. But it stretches *my* imagination to believe that those whites possessed settling intentions. The whites converted the black and brown victims of their immemorial deceit, by creating a mugging-mystique of mythological racial absurdities, into incoherent, senseless, pathetic sub-humans, totally dependent on the white Lord of the Land, Tarzan, God's earth-bound muscle, who harnessed the raging land and its untrainable 'creatures' to lay it all at the feet of white womanhood on a pedestal.

A fanciful world of make-believe gradually became ingrained as an intrinsic component of the white genetic mentality. With racial vanity as a yardstick, with knowledge gleaned from Britain's history books, every white man in Africa and Asia became ten times larger than life. They were supposedly adventurous, courageous, stiff-upper-lipped, gallant, heroic, valiant, chivalrous and blue-blooded. 'Chinese' Gordon of Khartoum, Livingstone, Clapperton, Speke, Rhodes, Thomson, Burke and Wills, etc., and for ever more. The exploits of these white historical heroes gradually became intertwined and interwoven with the exploits of mythical comic-book heroes. So much so, that in the miasma of British history, the line between fact and fiction is totally indistinguishable. Notice that these white he-men died 'heroically'. Was there ever any white man in Africa or Asia who did not die, usually grossly outnumbered, 'heroically'? Interestingly, these showcase whites of Empire have a class-equivalent in British fiction of that period. Lord Peter Wimsey and Sherlock Holmes, with their razorblade upper-class cunning intellects, exposed and undermined the so-called inferior intellects of the lower classes.

The white orchestrations, performed in Africa, need review. In their haven of galloping natives, negative names like 'darkest Africa' or 'the dark Continent' were introduced by those people who never saw light in anyone black, and relagated those ape-like, empty headed, physical blacks into paper men and women. Those labels were used essentially to denote the helplessness of the blacks and browns by conjuring up a pile of sluggish, impervious bricks, in order to perpetuate the myth of nonwhite inferiority. When the pick-up band of contemporary white journalists arrived to make today's scene, with the same patronizing droppings of their forefathers, being unable to stretch their limited imaginations, the white juke-box repeated the same white negative attitude towards blacks and Asians, the same hallucinations, the same labels.

In an *Evening Standard* article of March 1980, Max Hastings admitted to that biased negative approach, in an article which revealed what white journalists, in general, had traditionally omitted from their reports:

> . . . Ho ho. Those of us who have reported from Rhodesia over the years, have come to take so much for granted; the chatter about 'the munts', 'the Kaffirs', 'the indigenous' that would cause embarrassment in Enoch Powell's parlour; the weight of hatred and contempt for anyone who has voiced disagreement with 'the struggle to preserve standards'; the courage and enterprise of the farmers and industrialists; the absence of culture; the startling physical beauty . . .
>
> In the past 15 years, there has been much talk in Rhodesia about the standards that Mr Smith and his army have allegedly fought to maintain. It is true that this country and its white people are marvellously clean, because there has always been an army of black workers to keep them so. The whites are reasonably law-abiding, hard-working, disciplined and hospitable . . .
>
> For ten years, there has been a growing and finally total lack of concern among most whites about the circumstances in which blacks have died in the war. Black civilians killed in crossfire were simply scribbled in the casualty lists as 'curfew breakers'. Thousands of blacks were moved from their own areas into 'protected villages', often without the slightest provision for the basic necessities of life. In some cases, their new homes were merely map references in the bush.

I discovered the tricks of Britain's white journalists in Africa, showing how these Sons of Empire became heirs to disaster. In an article entitled 'Tolerated guests', in *New Society* November 1977, alluding to their methods of story-discovery, I wrote:

This is Zambia. Lusaka the capital. The capitals within the capital are the bars. Here at hotels like the Intercontinental on Haile Selassie Avenue, the hookers have congregated – not girls, but the journalists who, preferring the title 'foreign correspondent,' concoct the news. They are awaiting the imminent arrival of India's General Prem Chand, UN special representative. The British Commissioner-Designate for Rhodesia, Lord Carver, follows shortly.

Twelve years ago, foreign correspondents decided that the Smith regime was about to fall. According to these experts at cutting their cloth to suit and the front page, it still is. 'Noise proves nothing,' said Mark Twain's Pudd'nhead Wilson, 'often a hen who has merely laid an egg cackles as if she had laid an asteroid.' The same could be said of foreign correspondents. It is, after all, due to an ingrained fanatical desire to obtain a scoop, that some blatantly exaggerate and transmit distorted facts. Not surprisingly, 'big things do have small beginnings,' especially if the small thing started off in the hands of some foreign correspondent.

This is the world of the foreign correspondent: filled with telex and alcohol. Jet lag, credit cards and craziness. Shallow, superficial and super-exciting. Super-lies, super-cliques, super flams and super ego – the Super Tramp.

Some of the most notable of these adventure story writers abide by the oldest rule in journalism: 'Never muck up a good story with facts.' The *Daily Telegraph,* considered to be the worst fantasiser by many journalists out here, is nicknamed, 'the west's *Isvestia.*'

A current tale going around the bars is of the correspondent who was scouting in a light aircraft over Cabinda, Angola's oil enclave, when a MIG shot past him – at about 1,200 mph. His account of this split second happening was: the steely eyes of the Cuban pilot glowered hate at *me*. His bared teeth held a Havana cigar in a vice-like grin. He flew towards me with guns spitting violence . . . This earned him a week's detention in the local gaol.

Here in Lusaka, because of the fluid political situation in Rhodesia and South Africa, rumours abound and spread like wildfire. Journalists play a significant role in the spreading. Recognising this, African governments force-feed them, like Strasbourg geese, with stories they want highlighted. Smith,

Kaunda and General Amin are pastmasters at this game. To get the correspondent, officials bait the hook with tempting stories: 'Nkomo is secretly meeting X.' The news spreads suddenly. Foreign correspondents descend like vultures from all over Africa to get a bit of the free information. For a day – or a week – they circle lazily (in ever-decreasing circles from bar to bar) and then go on to their next 'story.' Their readers may be left baffled, but the bars and the airlines go smiling all the way to the bank.

In investigative journalism there is a fine line between reporting and spying. Foreign correspondents are tolerated guests. They are entitled to comment but not encouraged to interfere with the sovereignty of a state. Hence the dearth of hard information.

By far the largest percentage of stories about the Rhodesian guerrilla war are planted from inside Rhodesia itself. Foreign correspondents are invited by the Smith regime, to show that the government has nothing to hide. A lot of native bar-bound correspondents fall for this. According to many correspondents in Lusaka, invitations to visit Rhodesia are extended to those reporters who have 'shown some sympathy' with the Smith regime. In that way, some supposedly free-thinking foreign correspondents may unwittingly become mouthpieces for the Rhodesian government. That being so, news from Rhodesia can only be one-sided and should be taken with a pinch of salt.

This is reinforced by the fact that no western correspondent has been permitted to enter any ZANU or ZAPU camps (freedom fighters opposed to Smith). Nor have they been allowed to view the fighting going on from the territories of the frontline states surrounding Rhodesia. These no-go areas are Tanzania, Mozambique and Zambia. Thus, lurid descriptions of border fighting lose their credibility.

Conversations with some correspondents yield little information of any real substance. What becomes increasingly clear is that any acquaintance with local population is lacking. As one travel weary American journalist said, 'I would like to know where the workers live.'

At Lusaka's Intercontinental, the ambience seems to be tainted with the colonial mentality. It appears to be a bastion of a bygone era. Anyone could be forgiven for thinking that the atmosphere of

Evelyn Waugh's *Scoop* was alive and thriving in Lusaka. At the sun's zenith, the swimming pool is filled with the noisy, uninfectious laughter of expatriates' wives – whiling away the length of their husbands' contracts. (There seems to be an unwritten rule that black and white must not swim at the same time.) Meanwhile, lunching correspondents huddle at the Makumbi bar and restaurant overlooking the swimming pool, gaping lecherously at the various bikinied body shapes. Waiters scurry around them, bearing exotic drinks, 'I say,' booms one correspondent, with that nasal accent that sorts out the bosses from the workers. He delivers his order with a reminiscent condescension. It is precisely this kind of attitude which has brought Rhodesia and South Africa staring full face at violent confrontation.

Meanwhile, here at the Intercontinental there may be a question of sovereignty. Outside this place, Zambia – indeed, black Africa – is independent.

So, why were the British people so shattered by the news that Robert Mugabe was to be the Prime Minister of Zimbabwe? Were they ripped off by the twisted news of their media? They were in fact being plunged into history and not being given news. Any black man, if asked, could have told them, at the very beginning, that the information white journalists trafficked from their hotels, would be white propaganda and not news.

Consequently, the white British journalistic vacuum-cleaners, so sure of a white Rhodesian victory, because it was a British-type army, weighted the news of the war in Zimbabwe against the black Zimbabweans, finally outsmarting themselves. For years the British public with Empire mentality-infested psyches, were sucked in by the con-penmanship of their media illusionists, who impressionistically painted a daily death toll of how many black 'terrorists' had been slaughtered by Rhodesia's sanguinary white immigrants. All in all, if one totalled, in the entire war, the number of freedom fighters supposed to have been killed by the white British representatives, those white butchers would have demolished the lives of at least three times the number of black freedom fighters that actually exist in the whole of Africa.

Moreover, the war was fought on two fronts, each supporting

the other, each needing the other. The first front took place in Zimbabwe itself. The second front was in Britain, where the white British press constantly placed into the white public mind, the 'wrongness' of the black African struggle and the 'rightness' of the white Rhodesian immigrants, by artistically and skilfully conjuring up memories of the past, as also highlighted by James Morris in *Pax Britannica*:

> The Indian Mutiny, too, had tainted British attitudes towards coloured people. It had occurred in 1857, and was one of the few imperial events which had gone into the English folk-myth, on a par with the marriages of Henry VIII, say, or the murder of the princes in the Tower. It was a favourite horror story. The British saw it in terms of cowering white ladies in fetid cellars; goggle-eyed Indians, half blood-man, half lustful, creeping unawares upon sweet English children in lace pantaloons; the massacre of innocent hostages, ambushes, orgies, treachery.

The brainwashing continued with the viciousness of the black freedom fighters, as opposed to the disciplined militarism of the whites; the glory of the Selous Scouts, as opposed to the perversion of the Patriotic Front; how the Patriotic Front had intimidated every black and brown man in Zimbabwe, while the white army of bandits spent enormous amounts of money and manpower, protecting black lives. Where in history has any white power structure ever protected black lives?

The white man became the black man's burden, when some British individuals and companies (with the British government, as usual, mouthing denials of knowledge), created a new Hollywood, with panorama effects thrown in. The extravaganza, blockbusting motion picture in Africa was created, *The Sanction Busters,* made along the lines of *Gone With The Wind*. At black protests, the whites told the blacks to 'Go to the wind for an answer'. And they did, in the shape of an African racial truism, which is: no white man negotiates with a black man, unless he has been made to. Consequently, the white Rhodesian struggle, to hold on to what was not theirs in the first place, resulted in the London Lancaster House Conference. The black Zimbabweans had brought them to their knees; and there being a very fine line between greed and defeat, the whites lost everything.

At the beginning of the black Zimbabwean War of Independence, Ian Smith's white assassins were described by Britain's journalists as the 'illegal regime', for a whole five minutes. And they quickly introduced positive and negative mind-bending imagery, so as to seduce Britain's white majority into siding with their homicidal cousins infesting a black man's country. A land in which the blacks had repeatedly stated that whites were more than welcome to remain, *as equals*. But the white definition of 'equality', as the world knows, is completely based on a set of immoral morals, which black people refuse to understand and will never come to terms with. With some racialistic foresight and harmony through 'the old school tie', the British government and Britain's media literally overnight massacred the term 'illegal' replacing it with the positive image of 'security forces'. Meanwhile, blacks, who were Zimbabwe's rightful owners, suddenly became 'terrorists', 'guerrillas', 'bandits', 'murderers'. All of which perpetuate an artistic negative image. But what is noteworthy, is that literally none of Britain's journalists reporting from the white man's homefront in white Rhodesia, truthfully described Zimbabwe's black fighters the way they should have, which was 'freedom fighters', especially if that regime was as illegal as the British government claimed. Or were they 'legal in their illegality' which blacks and Asians know is the white man's traditional definition of black equality with whites.

Furthermore, in their genetic wish for a white victory, white Britain accidentally forgot to stop and think that the white negative reporting of the blacks' rightful struggle for Zimbabwe was being noticed, absorbed and remembered by Britain's blacks and Asians; who were themselves being reported by other white journalists, in very much the same negative terms. The only horrendous fact for whites was that through the universality of communications systems, biased reporting against blacks is a boomerang that will always return. For *Britain has finally colonized herself but she has yet to realize it.* The victor's toll.

Let us take a look at some of the negative reporting on Zimbabwe that invaded the British atmosphere:

The Sunday Times, August 1980: 'Officials report that many tribesmen and guerillas are unhappy to hear ministers urging *white farmers* to remain on the land.'

The Times, April 1980: 'There are still about 30 British soldiers in Zimbabwe helping to train former *Zanla* and *Zipra guerillas* who are being integrated with the *Rhodesian security forces.*'

Guardian, February 1980: 'Five black civilians have been killed in crossfire between *security forces* and *Patriotic Front guerillas*, a Rhodesian military spokesman said yesterday. Two *guerillas* and one *white security force* member also were killed he said.'

Evening Standard, February 1980: 'As 22,000 *guerillas* at assembly points all over Rhodesia voted today.'

Daily Telegraph, April 1980: 'Four men, including a *white security forces* member, held by Rhodesian police concerning a hand-grenade attack on Mr Mugabe's suburban Salisbury home, have been released.'

Michael Raeburn, author of *Black Fire! Accounts of the Guerilla War in Rhodesia* published in 1978, was consciously or subconsciously image manipulating when he wrote: 'But despite periodic bouts of fierce fighting against *Rhodesian security forces* during the latter half of the decade . . .'

Due to the oppressive weight of the British press image-inventing, the illegality of the white Rhodesian regime who were racing against time on a non-stop black Roman Holiday, was strategically lost sight of, by whites only. But the black question is, whose security were those white-led forces securing? 'Security', in a political sense, suggests a 'just cause' which made the misnamed 'terrorists' appear to be the impediment to the peace Britain so loudly proclaimed she wanted. So whose interests were they really 'securing'? Obviously it was the only people with any real material interests in that black country – white Rhodesian immigrants and their white British 'kith and kin'. Consider it, consider it carefully, bearing very much in mind the interminable history of Africa's blacks at the terroristic hands of white immigrants.

The white image-manipulation of blacks continued. 'Guerilla' as it stands, gave no political credibility to the black Zimbabwean struggle. And 'guerilla' as opposed to 'security force' implies that the black cause is not legitimate. But the 'nationalist guerilla' or 'freedom fighter' tells the world that Zimbabwe's blacks have a 'just cause' and the white immigrant opposition is the 'impediment', to their rightful rights. Especially when those white immigrants were internationally declared to be 'illegal' by Britain. In this context, the long arm of the white law suddenly became short, for blacks.

The white Rhodesian immigrant's struggle exploded the white mendacity of the 'protecting Zimbabwe's blacks' policy. That fabricated fantasy ultimately proved to be Africa's white parasites' jamboree; which reveals a self-evident truth in African perspectives: the more they *protect* whites from blacks, the more they are going to have to destroy blacks. So keep your peekers trained on the white illegal immigrants in South Africa, which will ultimately, universally be known as The People's Republic of Azania.

6
In Cold Storage

Let me tell you something you may not know.

The upheavals which happened on the darker streets of Bristol 1980, Brixton and Southall 1981, were the initial kick-out against a variety of second-rate white offerings, by Britain's black and Asian home-grown youth and their young white allies. Realistically, the relegating of Britain's blacks and Asians to second-class citizens also forcefully relegated their second-classness to permanency. But 'aspiration' for blacks and Asians being just a juicy idea, a promised-land ideal gave activity to the realization of black and Asian youth that they were just as colonized as their parents who were born in the ex-colonies.

But there exists an iron-hard streak of aggression in Britain's black and Asian youth, who were, ironically, also cultured to understand the white British mentality. They were born here, nurtured here, almost totally by their parents and, finally, belong here. That is why they, like much of white youth, refuse to accept blindly what many whites consider to be their lot in life. They will rightly fight, and aggressively, for their just rights. Make no mistake: the black experience has taught them so.

Moreover, through the most gruelling, agonizing and shameful white dismissal of young black ability, by ignoring their talent, coupled with the white discounting of the reality of their presence, the white body-politic was shattered to hear the young blacks and browns powerfully proclaiming, 'We are black and we are British, and we have a right'. The white body slumbered on, as their politics began. And they, peeking through their lace curtains of black inferiority, only saw what they had programmed themselves to see, which was 'immigrants', and 'coloureds' (which colour?) in the guise of black and brown bodies. And from the White Band of Light and Purity there arose a resounding, but resourceful, declaration: 'They have an identity crisis', as they moved in their sociological first line of attack. Not yet realizing that that so-called black 'identity crisis' was white and the destructive white behaviour toward blacks.

It is you, the white Prince of Evolution, who are the crisis, through your own infinite attempts to manipulate black and brown peoples the world over; and having failed in that outlandish quest, you then tried to counterfeit the black identity by framing them into a 'coloured' facade. That failed too. For what the Superwhite all-brained-body had clean forgotten in his frantic and endless 100-metre dash to make himself rich (a euphemism for black and Asian agony), was that knowledge, in its majestic glory and purity, *has* no colour, but its users do.

Moreover, knowledge is infinite and has no owners. So why are Britain's white earthlings still utilizing the identical sabotaging caricatures, created by those piratical great white fathers of Empire, on black and Asian people today? Or are Britain's whites really saying that human intellectual progress is a special preserve of whites only? But what is also self-evident to the black and Asian condition is that knowledge of the white behavioural progression *is* a special preserve to them.

Over the centuries, black and Asian peoples have taken in-depth courses on the Evolution of the White Psyche, watched the creation of white fantasies, and seen the addition of their wealth to Britain's.

They watched white men arrive, instantly claiming they had 'discovered' them, to the hinge-creaking extent that they only truly existed when propagated by whites. The holy rollers went along for the ride too and blessed those whites as they tried to flatten black and Asian skulls into the shapes they wanted. But they never broke their spirit and never broke their wills; despite reducing the men into beasts of burden and degrading their women, by rape, into ravaged victims of white lusts. Those violent exploits became a British way of life, an attitude, an accepted behaviour requiring no more consideration. It became *the* attitude, *the* accepted behaviour.

But consider this: why have Britain's whites not yet thought themselves out of their own self-inspired present-day racial dilemma? Do they not think this is the opportune moment to begin equalizing with the blacks and Asians, and stop dictating to them? Or is it because the Establishment has for so long dominated dictatorially their own victims of lust, the white working classes, with the result that negotiation with their considered lowest forms of human life is always out of the question?

Yes, black and Asian people have watched Britain's whites inflicting injustices, with pity in their eyes; but the flame of defiance is constantly being upheld by another little item, which is, they all possess through political reality, historically transferred exacting memories. What black and Asian people have never forgotten, with constant white British physical reminders, is the white man's alternative Darwinian conqueror's ethic, 'suppression of the considered weakest'. With this opportunistic measure, British history is laced with the black and brown human debris of their sanguinary exercises. Black and Asian people have memories.

They remember that the answer for any problems of the colonized was punishment. The answer *any* human being ever wanted to *any* problem, was a solution. Those whites decided that their only solution to any problem, at home and abroad, was punishment. That is, until black and Asian people themselves became the problem, by merely demanding their rights. The Establishment felt threatened and white genocide of black and Asian people was repeated as their Final Solution.

In the global testing-ground of human manipulation, subjugating one's own is infinitely more manageable, more permanent and ultimately more effective than dominating another. The magnificent imperial weakness lay in her attempt permanently to dominate other races, made intractable by the startling fact, the universal racial victim's axiom, that they will ultimately see through all carpet-covered perjuries, and finally, they not only will not, but cannot, accept for ever the domination of themselves by another race. All racial genetic instincts, under that type of subjugation, are potently combustible and are always in opposition to it – in this instance, whites. Which is also a fact which determines the future result of the decimation of the Afrikaaner, through that genetic time-device, with the helping-hand of Her Majesty's Government built into the psychogenesis of the black Azanian majority. And the whites will weep.

It should be no surprise that Britain's black and Asian attitudes have hardened by the constant rejection of their grievances. Britain is now forced to recognize that she has on her hands a resolute people who have for centuries been an essential part of the British community; who have done more than enough to justify a slice of the national cake, who have weathered degrading treatment just for being here in Britain, and just for being. A people who have withstood a superabundance of racialistic attacks from the moment they landed, and who saw many, not all, of Britain's whites as onlookers of injustice, failing to see black and Asian ill-treatment at the hands of whites; a people who interminably walked away from confrontation, with the result that many whites proclaimed they were the cause of it, will not again walk away from confrontation, at the cost of losing, as they have usually lost in British hands, their human rights and their lives.

The question now is: will the rule of the cosh be the last gasp in black and Asian lives? For an answer, the history of Britain's treatment of black and Asian people from the day they landed on the shores of this 'sceptred isle' thundered NO.

Britain's blacks and Asians and their white allies could see it; black and white America, having felt it, could see it; black Africa, still feeling it; could see it; the Afro Caribbean peoples, who had tasted it, could see it; the Asia still paining from the effects of it, could see it; even the Soviet Union, strangely, could see it; in fact, everybody in the world could see it. The white British psyche was shattered by it.

Having advertised continuously, internationally, her much envied social situation of 'peace and tolerance', through the 'tranquil harmony' of the most homeostatic society on earth, she smarted from the torrid weight of international derisive opinion, grating the 'pride and glory' of the Britannic trident, blasting to bits the idea that she was free from social revolution. The United Kingdom, protesting her innocence, reluctantly re-entered the mortal world.

That grand euphemism for British political opportunistic expedience, 'public confidence', suffered a set-back through the uncomfortable knowledge that the governing powers had no answer for Britain's psychic pain.

In reaction, the tradition-bound white British soul buried its head back into the dust of its worshipped historical glory. Technologically, Britain is an advanced country but socially she is stagnant. Through her adulation of yesterday's glorious exploits, she momentarily re-emerged from her love of her own history books to be sustained by her imperial pride.

But the inquisitive chattering telecoms, reducing the world to seconds, prevented the sweeping of Britain's international humiliation under a carpeted facade: shattering the fantastic assumption that, universally, Britain is seen the way she sees herself. That shock in turn jolted her SAS-brain cells, which had always supported her justification for her self-image. As St Paul's, Bristol, rocked the air of stability, Britain asked why?

Why? What a late question. How could she have failed to notice the reasons for the street disturbances which lay in her doings of her own deeds. In the rhyme of her accepted reasonings, she could. Glory. Glory. Glory. She had fed her own people on it and fed other races as negative palliatives to them. Thus enabling them to forget their own class-position through what they saw as positive promotion. Her people believed it through encouraged amnesia which negated the reality of British failures, for instance, the violence of her administration of other races. Which explains another white shock on hearing blacks' and Asians' allusions to their country's colonial violence; and further explains the present-day instinctive disbelief of black and Asian cries of white injustices in Britain. Programmed excuses. What Britain had kept in cold storage suddenly sizzled spontaneously onto the delicate balance of Britain's streets.

Moreover, it was the pain of centuries which was the force behind the black and Asian reaction, equally and opposite to the very white shock. The stalking contest of the black and Asian probability, against the white-considered impossibility, now over, reinforced that the possibility of a major street disturbance is always solidly and latently potent for the future.

Britain's black community knew it, the Asian community knew it, their white friends also knew it. Even Britain's tourists commented upon it. But the sluggish white body-politic was stunned by it. *Brixton*. Ironically, the way it was 'stunned' by the inevitable demise of white Rhodesians; as it will also be 'stunned' by the guaranteed defeat of white South Africa.

Britain's black and Asian communities have always known their own their own minds; a fact which whites refused to believe, and which with hindsight never mattered. Black and Asian actions in Britain have severed the arteries of arrogance, steering white thought, proving that racial vanity cannot answer theirs or any racial dilemma. That is the philosophy behind the specifics.

Nevertheless, some loaded elements with nothing to lose, with a class identity crisis, colloquialized as skinheads; low-riding the streets, overwhelmed by a racial compulsion to test that slammer: 'that a nation is as strong as its considered weakest'. This physical arm of a racist reaction considered Southall to be the place to slap, to keep themselves happy. Wrong again. The slap-happy skin-beaters met a brown wall of stone, which stoned them. And they were blinded by the light, that it was themselves who were always the weakest and blacks and Asians were always the stronger, as their identity was always concretely intact. The identity of anyone *aware* of being victimized is always clear cut.

The message is beginning to hit home; the more white racists attack black and Asian people, the more they will have to defend whites, and in their defence, their need to exaggerate and fabricate will be greater, in order to justify their dearth of solutions. A diversionary tactic. Anyone who cares enough can see that white British injustice only creates a quivering and latent potential for rebellion in black and Asian people. In another sense, life is a mixture of secure insecurities, but security must be the larger element, being the very essence for internal stability. Black and Asian stability is assured by their situation.

Media methods reflect outmoded practices of centuries, by continuing to play the bad-mouth, bad-nigger music, as is reflected in their reports of Britain's street disturbances in 1981, using positive and negative racial images. So when does a riot become a rampage? When the participants are all white.

Notice the style of the reporting and headline language on the back page of the *Guardian*, 27 July 1981:

POLICE CLASH WITH MOB IN LAKE DISTRICT

Police battled with about *1,000* motorcyclists and scooter riders armed with *axes* and *coshes*, in Keswick on Saturday.

The confrontation took place at about 10 pm at the lakeside car park, on the outskirts of the Lake District town and on the shore of Derwentwater. Police carrying riot shields moved in to prevent the youths marching on the centre of the town.

The youths, who came from many parts of the country, attacked with *bricks, slates* and *bottles*. The Century mobile theatre, where nightly shows are given for holidaymakers, was badly damaged, along with an ice-cream stall and parking kiosks. A parked caravan was burnt out.

Fourteen youths were arrested, mostly charged with offences under the Public Order Act, and one policeman was treated in hospital for leg injuries.

Gangs of youths had been riding around the Lake District during Saturday, but police called in reinforcements from a wide area in the evening when the riders converged on Keswick. *Some of the youths were said to be armed with petrol bombs.*

The Mayor of Keswick, Mr Claude Metcalf, described the attack as *pure vandalism* and said that everything in the car park that could be broken had been broken. There was no glass left in the theatre, and its two bars had been completely wrecked. [My italics]

Now for the *Guardian's* front page of 11 July 1981:

BRIXTON YOUTHS GO ON RAMPAGE AS RIOTS SPREAD

Rioting erupted again in Brixton, South London, last night hours after Lord Scarman closed the first phase of his inquiry into the *riots* in April.

Several hundred youths, predominantly black, gathered in the streets and shop windows were broken, shops looted and two police cars burnt. [My italics]

The slippery truth is out. A rampage becomes a riot when the participants are *predominantly black*. Blowing the guts off the cover-up that the racial bad-mouthing blockbusts the grey cells into seeing the accepted hypocrisy: that the artful language of headlines is a blind brother's game, being the foundations of their ground rations. Will the Rule of the Media, be the Exaggeration in all our lives? Or will they only go for Soul?

Politics is all about the art of timing. In recognition of this obvious fact, which obviously was not obvious to some who timed their politics at the wrong moment, about the wrong people and with the wrong intentions in mind, the evasion philosophy strolled in carrying a white-tonic: 'Our brainless black victims are totally incapable of standing up for themselves, it is all the doing of extremists and outside forces which have stirred them all up.' Remember the words of that 'great white disappointment' Ian Smith and the black Zimbabwean nationalist struggle. Those whites said it was the work of communists. In any victor/victim situation, how can any 'outside influence' be responsible for the victor's racial tunnel vision, especially when the 'victim's rebellion' takes place? Based on a white belief of black incapability 'the powers that be' could not admit that they had ignored a reality staring them in the face. Prevarication tangoes in. They preferred excuses, suggesting that if they need to rely on excuses in those situations, they had no answers; and it further means that they themselves had no understanding of the problem in the first place, which raises the question, *what is leadership?*

Leadership to any problem only exists if the so-called leaders themselves, in the context of that particular problem, understand the problem. Which then gives the followers the confidence that the outcome from the leaders' solution-policy is well founded.

A persecuted minority is a trembling united mass. In order to change direction, a major obstacle is the force that gives it the reason to do so. In the act of changing direction, every single component, consciously or subconsciously agrees. That is why black and Asian people do not need a Moses or a white liberal or the so-called left-wing extremists or left-wing liberal friends, to show them the way. Blacks and browns already know, by courtesy of the white opposition, in which direction to go. This action is called Spontaneity. The reaction that does not understand it is called Excuses, which stems from the ignorance of those whites who suggest blacks and Asians are incapable of action. Therefore, the propounded argument of why black and Asian people have reacted, through being 'stirred up by outside forces' was a lie before it left the mouths of the people who said it. But what constitutes the definition of the victim's rebellion? And when it happens, do you recognize it? Liverpool?

In an attempt to blow the guts out of Britain's 'riots' shock, the hunt for palliatives began with that infamous British word, which time had institutionalized through its constant repetition. The evasive white soul singers struck up this greasy refrain: 'Inquiry, Inquiry', let's give them an 'Inquiry', which, it was hoped, being the natural British way of doing things, would institutionalize the problem. This devious mechanism usually helps the controllers in any situation not to see what they don't want to see, which is the wood, the very core of the society's anxieties, preferring to it the trees of pretence. Result, the drive for answers through clear alternatives was lost, the moment the word 'Inquiry' was heard. In Britain, everyone is fully aware what happens to an inquiry, even before the inquiry begins. Nothing. Then, the grand Britannia recommences the same course, until the next storm.

Consequently, if the minds who set up the Scarman Inquiry don't know the reason why the disturbances happened, they then have admitted that they have psychologically, in themselves, demolished all the indicators over three decades which pointed to the explosive possibility of it. How can the black and Asian community trust the understanding of those minds they are inquiring into? Which informs us the inquirers themselves hold a view of Britain which is light years in distance different from the view held by those being inquired into.

Conclusively then, the Scarman Inquiry failed the moment it was announced. Lord Scarman's statement, 'Trust me and you will not be betrayed' to the black and Asian communities would not have been said if he had understood the following which appeared in the *International Herald Tribune* of 20 April 1981:

Without Representation

Now that more than 40 per cent of the country's nonwhites are born in Britain, they find it irritating to hear their troubles described as an 'immigration problem.' They have the frustrated feeling that 'no one is representing us,' as a black driver said. There are no nonwhites among the 635 members of the House of Commons, nor are there nonwhites in positions of importance at Buckingham Palace or 10 Downing Street.

Offensive racial stereotypes that have long since disappeared from public view in the United States – cannibals, pickaninnies and shiftless black servants – still appear in British advertisements and cartoons, despite a government-sponsored educational campaign.

Sir David McNee, the London police commissioner, conceded that 'a multiracial society is putting the fabric of our policing philosophy under greater stress than at any time' in the past 150 years. With severe recession, national unemployment has climbed to 10 per cent; among the young and poorly educated in places such as Brixton, it may reach 20 per cent to 30 per cent.

Rejecting suggestions to increase public spending in the riot area, Prime Minister Margaret Thatcher said: 'Money cannot buy trust and racial harmony. Trust is a two-way business. No one must condone the disgraceful acts which took place. They were criminal.'

Mrs Thatcher's economic austerity policies – including rigid restraints on spending for social programs – have restricted service and facilities poor neighbourhoods had come to expect under the old Labour Party government.

'But beyond all that sort of thing, it is a question of attitudes,' said Courtney Laws, the leader of the Brixton Neighbourhood Association. 'You cannot imagine what it is like to be black in white Britain. The attitudes are going to have to change.'

Most significantly, notice the clear style of reporting. Propelling a message to our own media landscape-gardeners that their considered balance is biased against blacks and Asians. Which highlights the conclusion that they have no clear idea of the oceans of difference between balance and bias. With shears, rakes, and forks, they have dirtied a profession supposed to reflect the anxieties and true images of any society, biasing their balance with a racial edge, and tightening the noose around Britain's neck. So, if they shift their bias towards balance, it would help.

In that statement made by Lord Scarman, was he aware that he would not be believed? Most significantly, his integrity was never in question. But it was obvious he had not considered that the community he was dishing the soothing balm out to, had had many headaches before. They had experience of white Britain's racially biased tonic to go with it. It never worked. It is hopeless taking a painkiller, if the pain has not been correctly identified. If he knew where the pain lay, the first thing he would have done was not to make that statement. Since lawyers, like Lord Scarman, are experts on British history, presumably he is well aware of the pitiless inhumanities committed by whites against these people. Therefore, he must also have been aware what the black and brown attitude, with well-grounded lack of confidence in Britain's system, would be to the setting up of what they see as a meaningless inquiry. Black and Asian people need no inquiries, they need a result from previous inquiries. Hence the dishing out of palliatives is better given to the white majority, if they will accept it. What will satisfy black and Asian people are lashings of certainties. They need the certainty that their children will be given educational opportunities; they need, proportionately, a guaranteed slice of the employment market; they need the certainty that no one will burn entire black and Asian families to death in their homes; and a certainty that the fascism they also fought against, will be dealt with by the law uncompromisingly. Lord Scarman, however honourable his intentions may be, cannot *certify* any of these things. He cannot issue a certificate that *certifies* that black and Asian people walking the streets are *certain* that a cold blade of Sheffield steel will not be thrust into their bodies. That their women will never again be violated; their children will stop leaving school merely semi-educated.

Another reason why the inquiry is not needed, is because the governing powers have for years now decisively shown they have no alternatives; no alternative way of talking or an alternative way of understanding black and Asian people. The rub is, because they have used the same methods over centuries, they have no other way. The Scarman Inquiry is merely a sugar-coated pill for the white majority. Again, the Scarman Inquiry will fail because it is based on all the wrong assumptions about who black and Asian people are. As was seen in the insensitive way in which the inquiry was formed with its obvious balanced-bias toward white public opinion and its treatment of non-whites as naughty children. The cutting scalpel sliced the lies from a racial cover-up. If Britannia's black and brown nationals were being crudely and condescendingly treated in the full glare of her own people in Britain, what must have been perpetrated on their skulls in her out-of-sight colonies? The chicken of truth is beginning to come home to roost. The inquiry that is desperately needed is one which will enable whites to find out who the black and brown British really are. History is wrong. Blow black, blow brown to understanding into white British lives.

Furthermore, in the hunt for *underlying reasons*, that inquiry had no declared intention of consulting black and Asian women, who have held the black and Asian communities together since their arrival in Britain. In their considerations the inquirers are well aware that their colour, coupled with their gender, forces them a class lower. Therefore by attacking black and Asian women, they are attacking the very roots of black and Asian communities. This is a land of fine frying slick-talk, which dismisses the savagely cultural reality; that if white Britain cuts out black and brown roots, the danger for Britain is that a great big British black oak will fall down on white skulls. You may find this ominous, but so are the white's physical and moral actions to black and Asian people.

Finally, through historical experience right up to this very day the black community knows it, the brown community knows it, their white friends also know it; and the entire white majority suspects it, that the inquiry will fail to change anything. Whose interest is that in?

It is true that knowledge is power, but it is the black and Asian communities and their white allies that possess the powerful knowledge, that white palliatives are now black guarantees. It is serious to mess around with the possibility of black and Asian mass action. There has to be a massive amount of integrity in the message of the white. Anything else means the white man's mind is still stuck in the mud of historical assumptions; that black people will continue to tolerate the hot jazz of white hot air. It is time to face the music because this nation knows the score.

There are some motor-mouths in this nation who believe that political parties are there to make policy and find answers to the problems of the nation. What if the political parties themselves are the problem? What if I said, if every black and Asian voter were to join a political party it would change nothing? Who could believe it? The answer would be dependent on their position on the ladder of class, what they have to lose, and which party they feel best represents their interests. But what if all the parties spring from the same racial foundations? And do they respect the racial interests of the other Britain?

Racial interest which can be easily seen in the agreement they have when it comes to formulating practical, not theoretical, policy: i.e. has any party ever promoted the obvious, which is, Britain must fundamentally change the basis of her political attitude to black Africa and Asia? When it is realized that Britain has always been a one-race political party, with racial superiority attached, how could she ever hope to negotiate with those countries using *her* definition of the basis of the equality as the starting point? A state which has always represented a one-race interest, cannot possibly have any of her political parties representing anything other than what she represents.

Great Britain once had an Empire, to which more than one race belonged. Outside its white members, which of the others have you heard singing hosannahs of thanks, hollering the praises of Britannia and ploughing gospels of gratefulness for the golden opportunities she left embedded in their imperial memories? But there *is* agreement among them, reflected in the unwavering constancy of black and brown opinion in Britain today. Which word does that conjure up in your mind? The one in mine you know.

And the blatant truth you also know. Black and brown bodies were always used to nourish and support white interests. The old leopardess not only changed her spots, but the spotty infection increased into an ulcerated rash, resulting in a spot-less hide. Lest the spots can be identified, the cancer remains; blemishing the racial basis of each political party. Through the use of emotion as leadership, which created white Britain's racism in the first place, how do they now diffuse their emotional issue? Bertrand Russell, in his book *Power,* accurately explains the build-up:

> But the leader is hardly likely to be successful unless he enjoys his power over his followers. He will therefore be led to a preference for the kind of situation, and the kind of mob, that makes his success easy. The best situation is one in which there is a danger sufficiently serious to make men feel brave in combating it, but not so terrifying as to make fear predominant – such a situation, for example, as the outbreak of war against an enemy who is thought formidable but not invincible. A skilful orator, when he wishes to stimulate warlike feeling, produces in his audience two layers of belief: a superficial layer, in which the *power of the enemy* is magnified so as to make great courage seem necessary, and a deeper layer, in which there is a firm conviction of victory. Both are embodied in such a slogan as 'right will prevail over might'.
>
> The kind of mob that the orator will desire is one more given to emotion than to reflection, one filled with fears and consequently hatreds, one impatient of slow and gradual methods,

and at once exasperated and hopeful. The orator, if he is not a complete cynic, will acquire a set of beliefs that justify his activities. He will think that feeling is a better guide than reason, that our opinions should be formed with the blood rather than the brain, that the best elements in human life are collective rather than individual. If he controls education, he will make it consist of an alternative of drill and collective intoxication, while knowledge and judgement will be left to the cold devotees of inhuman science. [My italics]

The power syndrome Bertrand Russell refers to, can be seen in the confidence trick the Empire builders used on their own people, by taking the weight off their minds, accidentally helping them to forget their position on the almost unclimbable vertical ladder of class. By conjuring up the power of the enemy on a religiously fearful people, the myths they created about black people took on a new status, and the tales of 'Darkest Africa' with its marauding savage natives, cemented it, a rich colourful legacy of negatives, which contemporarily infests white British minds. Ask any racist the basis for his beliefs, the concoction you hear will not only be baseless but based-less on his intelligence. So powerful is the trick of confidence, if unquestioned.

Who built the misnamed British Empire? Yes, there was an Empire. White scheming provided the draughtsmen using black and brown bodies to build the draughtsmen's schemes. And true to his scheming Britishness he had already schemed in advance, to take all the credit for himself, where have we seen that one before? Everywhere the British have schemed.

In Britain's structured class system, where the ruler's schemes divert the attentions of the majority, inhibiting their vision to notice, they have always lost out. The fact is, the Empire belongs to races, who by right, inhabit present-day Britain. But if they insist on still calling it 'British' then they are admitting those people were British in the past and incidentally the parents of the ones born here, are still British. Such is the trick of thought. The British Empire was a misnomer. Three races built it but a minority of Britain's whites controlled it to use it for their own interests. This also explains the vast differences in the division of wealth in

Britain today. Why do some individuals disproportionately hold more than their needs while the vast majority hold infinitely less? Who, in real terms, reaped the rewards of other people's labours? This demonstrates the white working classes were always as colonized as black and Asian peoples. The unthinkable has happened. Imperialism has finally colonized itself.

Therefore, the political parties, by only representing white interests, have never represented the interests of Britain's far-flung ex-colonial constituents. They have still to 'discover' that their obvious contemporary duty is to re-direct their previous racial dishonesty, with recognition of the three-dimensional race situation in Britain today.

In the liberal race against time, to speak of the race-condition by solving that problem overnight, some friends of non-whites have already made the classical error of the 'uptights' solution', by asking them to join the political parties. No doubt it is extremely important that that decision must be left to individual choice. But remember, by retaining their foundations, reflecting a one-race nation, Britain's main political parties merely use black and Asian peoples by manoeuvring them in slightly different ways, for their own interest. This is known as 'Blighty's Sham' which is composed of: one party says 'Let's go back'; another says 'No, let's just avoid the minefields by looking both ways'; yet another says 'No, let's satisfy everybody'; and the final one says, 'Don't let us say anything we believe in'. All of whom use that Great Seal 'The British People' as their rubber stamp, to get into power and develop instant amnesia.

However, the confidence in their tricks has not worked on black and Asian people, noticeable in the activity of their absence in Britain's political life. The political skin-beating skin-users should recognize that their party constitutions in no way understand the constitution of the political party black and Asian people already belong to, created by the white racist Opposition. Also by the outright failure of Britain's political parties through not meaningfully demonstrating their oppositions to that Opposition; which means they readily agree with it, through their immigrating use of it.

Contextually, that old cliché, 'actions speak louder than words', is a lie. In British politics, inaction is everything, and the actions the parties have liberated underlie the activity of their words, while continuing to consider blacks and browns as a 'soft election touch'. Additionally, the black and Asian voters' natural reticence to join Britain's political parties and take their rightful place in British political life generates from their belief that they are shady set-ups, because they still do not reflect the interests of the other colour Britain. They are merely facets of elitism, proving that all oppressors shuffle in different guises, but they all look the same to the victim.

The Commission for Racial Equality is the off-shoot of a permanent tranquillizer mentality, a pre-dated programmed relief, erected in order to satisfy the programmed paranoias of the whites in their immemorial one-sided arguments. A permanent identity crisis. All nations are in a constant state of paranoia. With Britain's historical behaviour deeply rooted in your mind, is it any wonder that her paranoia has become a weapon to be used faithfully? Britannic paranoia evolves from a series of unacceptable possibilities. The unacceptabilities are, that black and Asian people are *not* inferior, that she no longer controls the universe, that she no longer possesses yesterday's political and material power, and she still needs black and Asian contributions. The possibilities are, all those unacceptabilities are true. And the unacceptable becomes the paranoia, but only for the majority.

Among Britain's whites there are two views of Britain. The view of the ruling class, who represent the past but who do not live in it, who opportunistically and politically identify a crisis, usually by 'developing' it and then feed that crisis into the identity of the nostalgia-ridden masses, thus forming the other view.

Moreover, this type of psychological trickery is used in the discussions of the white-considered racial crisis, which is supposedly due to floods of black and Asian immigrants, conjuring up the dilution of the 'quality and richness' of Britain.

The identity crisis I speak of, is based on a series of unacceptable possibilities. And in this land where whites have endlessly identified themselves with superiority, the phrase *Great* Britain becomes clear and understood. The entrance of 'inferior', black and brown peoples into Britain provides us with a clear picture of the 'superior' white man's politically devised dilemma of paranoia, and he splutters *'how can I identify with that?'* The possibility that those white-considered black and brown inferiors *are* his equals, is totally unacceptable. Their visible presence increases his paranoia, reinforcing the possibility that it is more than likely a probability. And because the idea is unacceptable to him, his paranoia remains. Until he understands that, the white man's identity crisis will also remain.

British governments without remedies for potential agitation, institutionalizes it with no answer at all. No answer is, 'Inquiries', Royal Commissions and institutions like the CRE. The institution the CRE replaced is reflected in its name. The government viewed two problems, with two institutions. By setting up the Race Relations Board separately from the Community Relations Commission, it encouraged the white majority to arrive at the view that blacks and Asians required a separate institution for a separate problem, because the crisis was only about them. The identification of the RRB as *the* institution specifically for their crisis, was given more validity through isolated instances which had previously occurred, e.g. the 1958 Notting Hill Gate street disturbances.

The white majority knew it. The black and brown community knew it and also knew the government intended it: to do nothing at all. Who has it satisfied? Those it was intended to satisfy; the institutionalized accepters followed by an institutionalized dismissal programme.

To begin with, the CRE is a platitudinal guarantee; guaranteeing that all black and Asian complaints will be cushioned by a built-in inactivity. It is carefully sculptured to sieve the heat out of black and Asian complaints, by being founded on an alien form of integrity, made certain by the exclusively white interest it represents. Being based on wrong assumptions about black and Asian people, the CRE was never in danger of losing the confidence of blacks and Asians. Because it never had it. So good for the white majority.

Moreover, the relationship between blacks and Asians on the one hand and whites on the other, has always been based on aggression and condescension. This is the guts of the racial bucket in Britain today. In going high disguised as a Commission, it went home to where it belongs. To the Great White Fathers who have timelessly infested their relationship between them and their victims with Commissions of Bad Faith. The perfidy of which is fortified by the fake-book finger artistry which required the necessity of several fangless Race Relations Acts. One should have been enough.

In relation to black and Asian people, white authority has a singular honesty. That is, by matching in opposition the workable against the unworkable. This tactic allows them visually to achieve the impossible: by appearing to be progressing when they are, in fact, standing still.

In cold storage is the white definition of progress. In cold relation to the black and Asian definition of progress, which can be seen clearly in the devious intentions intended, when forming Britain's Race Relations laws. With experience in mind, Britain's whites feel that progress has been achieved, because *they* appear to be progressing, and non-white people appear to have been conned. Whereas, black people aeons ago cut loose from that crumb-dropping white ideal, and have defined progress as: *no white attempt to deceive*. The black and brown sledgehammer demand is: if a law intended to scalpel racist practices is broken, by *anyone*, that deviant must be hammered by the full force of the law, irrespective of colour or class.

Moreover, racially misconceived conceptions, if they continue unchecked and are not revamped, will always produce other conceptions which by implication are themselves misconceptions. The result being a contemporary inability to conceive conceptions which can murder the original misconceptions about others. Therefore, misconception becomes the order of the day. Resulting in the attitude that assaulting the human rights of others, will solve the original misconceived ideas about that race. So what is the Pax Britannica? In this instance, it is the total belief in human rights. It also demands women and men with the courage, integrity and the ability required to conceive new conceptions for the actual make-up and realness of a multi-racial and multi-cultural British body politic. Carry on misconceiving. Or use imagination to conceive optimism through the belief in, and knowledge of *real* alternatives. Thought is food for black and white and brown grey cells, for it has no owners.

7

Prospects

And central to the Question of the black and Asian presence in Britain; evolving from a Message which hurricaned the Caribbean, ran slicing into Asia, razored the African continent, grooming the Opportunist's Ideal, thrusting impetus into the Tommy, who spoke of pastures of Britain's potent Spring, of the cowslip and the buttercup, with sparrows on the wing; and if you sail to England, where the greening meadows smile, 'neath the oak by the rivulet, where thee can rest awhile. Frantically, framing and falling apart, freezing into their brains, that Britain was an inviting frolic pad, with a hustle all the same. They'll never forget red rivers wept, shrieking 'remember the centuries before'; child carried the pain loud and strong, which white chose to ignore, the enslavement of their peoples and the agony of their suppress, honing memories of devastated families, fighting Hitler for the West. 'Tis deeply etched in the Soulful, 'tis deeply etched in blood, 'twas always etched in rebelling, 'gainst further carnage of white, red black mud. Britannia encouraged the feeling, in brown people from the East, who came for hopeful prospects, to the pretence of an explosive feast; as did her other black victimized, divided into Two, burning lashings of final midnight oils, the tropical air turned blue. But, not knowing, The Question would never be answered, as they climbed, clambered, chasing dreams castles are made of, to meet the people who built those castles, with care, with motive, tended with purpose of no rights at all, cutting the expectation out of the black and brown Prospects ball. 'I have a dream', said one of their men, 'we also have one too, and we were also wondering, if our dream will end up like you'.

Their agony was stamped in a single teardrop which began what was to come, tumbling down little brown faces, those tears etched the future, represented their past, dropping the Truth into their present, and the answer came out at last . . .

'LET'S REPEAT THE BLACK EXPERIENCE'.

Lay down, those hearts of auspicious death knells, of final condemnations, 'rivers of blood', 'swamping' imaginations to 'backs against the wall'. Lay dead imperial product, with unreasoning for a philosophy, the sum total of centuries of absence of thought. For your answer is a rockpile of nostalgia: 'Let's repeat our history.' The Past for the Future? Run down and rocket away, for your Nothing Machine is X'ed out.

I, for one, am not a doom-merchant. Those inhabitants exist on the wrong side of the tracks of peaceful co-existence. For the distance between imagination and unimagination is the chasm in the philosophy of understanding there *are* alternatives.

'Never in a thousand years' was the voracious and uncompromising philosophy of the dominator, of the 'white minority' illegal regime ruling a black *majority* with the rod of brutality, in that black country, Zimbabwe. Curiously, those whites, holding a graveyard of bloodying projectiles to fragment and lacerate black bodies, felt threatened by Zimbabwe's unarmed black residents.

Consequently, black majority-ruled Zimbabwe was the result of the white Rhodesian minority's bloody philosophy. Britannia's kith and kin have remained in Zimbabwe, with the ready and publicly voiced acceptance of Zimbabwe's black majority. Which announces the jackhammering irony of the racial reversal: for it is they, the blacks, who now hold the ballistics, for the defence of *all*

Zimbabweans. Through white Rhodesians' insatiable materialistic racist appetite, aided and abetted by British inhuman racial irresponsibility towards Zimbabwean blacks, the ultimate black victory was a phenomenally high price paid for in black and their white allies' lives. Those white Rhodesians who died, killed themselves before they were dead. They did so by being extortionate parasites. Flip open your fogged blindness and focus on this: all oppressors are conclusively victims of their own beliefs, by freaking themselves into the tyrant's dogma: Me. Me. Me.

Those whites, in order to remain, have had to pledge their allegiance to the office of the black Zimbabwean Head of State. This is reflected in their visible participation in all of Zimbabwe's institutions, thus safe-guarding their racial interests by being woven into the fabric of a multi-racial society. Additionally, like the black and brown British, they are also in a minority. Notice that the Zimbabwean black majority have not copped out of their racial responsibility for the human rights of white Zimbabweans.

This is a land of elitist ladders, where condescension is the rung of 'bad taste' busting into everything, culminating in class and racial bitterness. In 1980/1, when Britain's streets were dusted by racial disturbances, we learned something. That the kinetic energy of bitterness is a powerful ladder to hate.

Nevertheless, there are bronco white racists among Britain's white community who have amply physically and morally demonstrated their wish to see the black and Asian experience repeated. Amazingly, *a white majority are fearful of a black and Asian minority*. Paranoia of a Christian path?

Crucially, black and brown ears have been whipped and deafened by the silence of white principle, a casual evasive guest. Or are silent principles principally silent for racial reasons? Contemporary Britain's white majority have constantly given moral justifications for any white minority dominating black and Asian peoples, globally, vomiting out, 'They are not ready'. But Britain persists in conclusively excluding her black and brown community from being cemented into the fabric of her so-called multi-racial society. Where is the threat? Solitarily confined in the white paranoid knowledge-box.

Britain is a land of ill-facades, where her advertised image promotes a high-powered, nut-cracking black reality. In present-day Britain, black and brown thoughts are the results of white actions constantly honing their attitudes to resoluteness. But if a chump is one who makes a quarrel out of a debate, who is quarrelling over whose interests, while encouraging the other to debate the quarrel? And what is the quarrel all about?

So, let us light the lamp in *this* Land of Darkness.

The merchants of doom merely promote ominous doom laden theories of death and destruction. With power in the front of their political minds, and treachery in the back, they are nothing but self-centred stoned souls, stealing away from responsibility. There are other motor-mouths, of every kind, stamping out insincerities, declaring Britain to be a 'multi-racial society'. They, for whom honesty is a one-night stand, are merely dusting the air with ulterior racial opportunistic motives with a verbal larceny.

In a truly multi-racial society, there is only one answer that all races can live with: a collective solution. But 'Immigration', 'Repatriation' and 'Deportation', are the only answers which will satisfy those racists existing in Britain's white community, an answer which gives confidence to only one side.

And here is the black out. With callous, but expensive, silence, calling an ill-wind, perceiving it as a soft cannon-ball of sane argument, the silent majority enters. Using the psychological razor blade of moral reasoning, they slashed the 'in' from 'injustice' with a swingeing immorality, while their belief in the rights of others took a moral holiday. Few whites seem to have seen discrimination. Blindfolded justice was the measure of the Pax Britannica, a 'peace' washed in the agonized blood of black and Asian people. And since the morals of a country are simply a reflection of its past morality blowing into focus the injustice that is welcomed in the present. The silence of the white majority silently shouts their agreement with racial intolerance, racial degradation and inhumanity, while they turn their deaf ear to those white, black and brown freedom believers who have the courage, the principles and the belief in the human rights of others. The silence of deafness attempts to shout their belief in humanity into silence. But the black and brown British have memories.

There's a cloud of shame hanging over this land.

Silence is what some dreams are made of. There is an anchor of pain in the heart of humanity, mugging countless minds with the memory of others' silences, boosting them on never to forget.

Silence can also be a nightmare. In the present-day past time, the gassed-down bloodied sinews of another race forever stain the minds of Germans' wartime Silence, which also allowed the *devaluation* of the nationality of Germany's Jews. Silence seduced the fractionalization of millions of families worldwide. In Europe it resulted in the ever-living tragedy of broken up, emaciated, mangled bodies; a wealth of humanity busted by the silence of the fence-sitters, culminating in the decimation of a race, who just happened to be Jewish. It was called Fascism, and Silence, his bosom-pal, encouraged him. Their melted down bodies remind the victimized and the principled with the flame of belief in human rights. Jews have memories about Germans. Such is the price of silence.

Neville Chamberlain, British pre-war Prime Minister, flew back from Munich and announced, 'Peace in *our* time.' That is Silence.

The Holocaust of the Pax Britannica broke down the bodies of countless numbers of Africa's blacks and Arabs, and other black Africans in the Caribbean, along with the Asian masses. Silence not only guaranteed it, but silently swallowed it into Britain's history books which, in the balance of time, were transferred into Britannic pride. Strung out by story-telling.

History is what a nation wants remembered; with human expediency it predatedly leaves out pitiless inhumanities used on others; the searing blow-torch of future conscience.

The present is the history for tomorrow, and a reflection of yesterday. If it is considered that history is something to learn from and not live in, then it is sad to see how frail the human ego must be, to see people give in to their weaknesses.

Through the precedents set in history, it would seem that a nation with no obvious purpose for direction, such as Britain, in times of recession passes the buck of leadership, as a diversionary tactic, to those who use tactics to divert their own maladies. The Jews were the scapegoats for the Germans. Britain's black and Asian people are used for similar purposes. In this country, leadership is moribund due to using the same gun-boat solutions, never requiring alternatives.

It cannot be in the interests of British national stability for the Hitlerite syndrome to happen in Britain. The terrible consequence of the rise of racial brutality is that, if black and brown lives are continually threatened or demolished in Britain, the defence of white lives in Asia, Africa and the West Indies will be horrifically paramount. I, for one, do not want that and I cannot believe that any sane person does either. So blow out the after-glow.

The time will come, after the failures of Britain's whites to use principle in their stand for their famed belief in justice, that men in a thousand years will say that 'this was their finest hour of injustice'. There is a cloud of shame hanging over this land and compassion has become a stranger. It was completely cut down yesterday. Making tracks when the merciless warriors of elitism macheted in to divide and rule, thus ruling the divisions of the white majority; resulting in Britain's present-day degradation called class. Compassion is now ashamed, lingering and lurking in dark shadows of concealment. Whereas, humanity, in a moral sense, was mugged by inhumanity, in the out-of-sight territories of British colonies. Immorally, it returned home to the Foreign Office, with the empty corpse of humanity as a camouflage. Compassion was still in hiding in the basement of the Home Office. The two watered-down passions convened in the sweat-shops of the media, instantly emerging as an aiding chorus, loudly advertising Britain's veiled compassion. It is called propaganda. In the eyes of Britain's blacks and Asians, that is the white British definition of humanity. A back door man.

The foundations for the loss of humanity are rooted in the beginnings of Britain's present-day advanced technology, which demanded the crushing of anything and anyone who impeded its progress, for instance, the black Zimbabwean peoples; from Cecil Rhodes to Ian Smith. However, those non-white peoples of the world without previous necessity for industrialization, retained a large element of human compassion which still persists today. Verifying that a savage culture with a psychopathic technology is the weakness crushing the strength of the strong.

Ever since the 1980/1 British street disturbances, the question which has permeated the social atmosphere is: 'What can be done to improve race relations in Britain?' The traditional British answer of creating institutions to solve a problem, in this instance, is positively negative. Because it merely dresses up pessimism to appear in the bright plumage of optimism. But first let us look at a modern-day example which continues to cement the negatives in the white race attitudes toward black and Asian people.

Decolonization provides us with the ground rations for the continual pumping out of negative images of black and Asian peoples onto a white Britain, which never heard anything else or anything good about those people, and therefore has clearly always believed in their inferiority and gives them no reason to change those ideas. The blatancy of the racial undermining of black and brown ability, helped by courtesy of the racial vanity shown in the balanced racial-bias of the hack reporter, interviewing a Minister with the wishful, negative question/negative answer ingrained habit, about the impending handover to a black or Asian government. Successfully reinforcing the rampant myths about black and Asian people, forcefully cementing them into the psychogenesis of modern-day Britain. But this pathetic device has failed.

Traditionally, the British government's justification for remaining in power and control of any black or Asian country and their resources, was bedded in the principle of the Back-firing Caucasian Confidence Trick. Before independence, the mendacity is: 'There are not enough qualified people to take over the country.' It backfires. Considering Her Majesty's Government, the Executive Controller of, say, India, for well over two centuries, why were there not enough 'qualified people'? It can only point to the savage and malicious intention to create a form of government that would be perpetually dependent on Britain's white administrators. Or was it because they wanted a white British social and political infrastructure?

Britain's definition of 'good government' is recognized by its total similarities to Westminster; taking no consideration of the differences of their culture and social values. All of which is based on a white crisis of identity, for they consider *identity* has value, when it exists as a replica of their own.

Whites who want a non-white government or non-white peoples

to be like their own or like themselves, are implying that they want them to result as clones of their own, or themselves. But it does not have to be like that. There are some whites who are sure of their racial identity, and wish for the identity of black and brown British to remain intact. They do not feel threatened.

This confidence trick was arrested by Britain's blacks and Asians, when the Rhodesian, Ian Smith, justified his reasons for retaining power after he had declared UDI. He pointed to the 'white fact' that there were not enough 'educated' black Zimbabweans. This pale deceit put a spell on Rhodesia's white immigrants, giving them a little more confidence to buy a little more time before the inevitable happened. In Asia and Africa, have you ever noticed that that white commodity of buying 'a little more time' always results in the loss of countless black and brown lives? However, Robert Mugabe, and his governing personnel, all possessed their current qualifications at the time that Ian Smith, the white farmer, spat that raunchy hateful statement. Strangely, Her Majesty's Government and Britain's media listened to the race music of Smith, and chose to allow the British public to believe it, by not significantly denying it. Furthermore, the British government could not deny the excuse she herself had used in nearly every colony, that much Ian Smith thoroughly understood and used to good effect. Proving that the politics guiding white actions in Asian West Indies and Africa is a con-man's game, which always backfires. For the actions in Britain's politics had become ideas for black and brown actions, here and abroad.

Independence Day Celebrations provide another heaven-sent opportunity for more race-music of the negative kind, to an ever waiting white British public, who in turn justify their good fortune in their British nationality, stability and all that. The deed is about to be done and the British television news atmosphere is heavily laden with Sunday Righteousness. They, the Great British People, are about to *give* something away, for nothing. Their pride is very British. Most probably based on the 'magnificent' British gesture, taking place in front of their very eyes. And the nation tunes in to a trick. The commentator begins in earnest, piling on adjectives about the 'great British presence', from the days when white men tamed that country, and its peoples, giving them the benefit of

British administration, education, agriculture and so on. The beat in the Independence arena is up-tempo, which also allows him the opportunity to get in 'still backward' outside the towns. The new government is in for a 'very difficult time', rumours of 'dastardly deeds' in the villages, coupled with an impending '*coup d'état*'. The rugcutting continues with heavy emphasis on the fact that the new government cannot survive 'without British aid' – carefully leaving out that that aid normally amounts to probably about ten pence per citizen. And, more importantly, the commentator totally sideslips the burning question: 'How much profit has the United Kingdom made, while she was governing that colony?' The commentator now pauses, and immediately continues with something about 'the struggle' and 'not ready', 'Britain did her best'. The white waiting millions, watching their talk-boxes nod agreement. The 'Great' in Britain is once again justified; 'we ruled the world', as some white British workers begin to get ready for their night-shift, and a take home pay-packet of £58 per week. That, I suppose, is reality. And the Independence scene they have just witnessed? 'Well, that helps take my mind off nasty realities.' An amnesia drop.

The scene is made. The Great White Giver, Her Majesty's representative, is flicked constantly on and off the screens. The mugging details about another race continue. Soon the homebound audiences, are convinced that, literally, six white men ran the country, while the indolent natives were mere onlookers. But now that they are moving house, the natives are neckbreaking it to grab a piece of the action, for they only trusted the whites. But not each other.

The Giver, resplendent in his cockeyed power outfit, mounts the rostrum all the while giving the waiting white millions his best superior smile, while surrounded by those aliens; as the commentator quickly points out, 'doing their funny dances'. The Giver, with trained dignity, struts to the new Prime Minister. Meanwhile, in the foreground of the background, the commentator, with paper emotion, pans a run-down of the magnificent career of the Giver. 'Yes' he has had a somewhat 'rather devilish time', but he did finally bring the new leaders, who 'were practically at each other's throats', to see reason. At this point Great Britain is about to lose her newly-found friend. Sweet man sweet. The conquering Tarzans have returned to try and trust those restless natives, whose brains were always out to lunch. The White Power dance is on.

The hour draws near, then the 'fears' Britain's whites have been waiting for are pulled out of the twilight world of her dirty tricks pot. *The* statements that the white British peepers and flappers on the media beat are avidly hankering for are: 'they cannot run their country without whites', 'will the whites be safe?', 'will these peoples start killing each other?', all voiced with such professional conviction, that Britain's white millions immediately believe no other human effort in that particular country exists. Only white talent and ability exist. He can play it cool, because he has an audience of willing believers. Curiously, these British television commentators never find anything positive to report about that impending ex-colony, or about its peoples, which does not explain why there was a British presence there in the first place, and for so long.

Nevertheless, all the while the white celebrations charade is happening; Britain's blacks and browns, most of whom are expert white-watchers, harden their resolve. For the celebrations, which I presume are supposed to be a momentous occasion of great joy, as per normal, merely turn into another catalogue of white British derision of black and brown peoples. Which in turn, puts a little more of the non-white-inability negative-issue into ready-to-believe, white brain cells. And the show goes on.

The false moment of naked-con has risen. The Great White Giver, with insincerity plus a delicate hint of condescension thrown in, painted carefully across his face, mouths a 'moving out' speech, the Great Tenant then hands over to the Owners their 'borrowed' land back and neck-breaks it out of the country. But the con almost certainly backfires. Within days, the white British residents are rudely awakened. That ex-colony may need whites, the rub is, the whites they need are not necessarily British. Great Britain has just burnt two boats. One with the new independent country: the other, with the black and brown British, along with a minority of whites. There is no doubt that those ceremonies, or other events must happen and be covered by the British media. But the time for thoughtless racial reporting is long over. And delivering mythical negatives, attempting to undermine another race's integrity, is watched keenly by a young determined British, white, black and brown youth, who carefully record the negatives used on another race; but which are also used on themselves. An issue has been put on underhand methods, which the British government and the British media push abroad, by way of the many negatives they peddle at Asia, the West Indies and Africa. This will always have a domino effect on British race relations. The backfire is complete.

Moreover, in nearly every British colony, true to their racial bias, Britain's whites erected a set of race laws (written and unwritten) which practically deprives that colony's black and brown citizens of their land rights, education and equal opportunity. Where have we heard that before? And, as usual, those race laws were always biased towards whites.

The smart stuff is repeated. Back home in Britain, where 'fair play' is the name of the game, the Race Relations laws, with colonial experience of skin-beating and separate development, are biased towards whites by carefully omitting the naked power of the law (which in the colonies was carefully woven in), even when a racist white deed is clearly blatant and legally proven. The offender, if white, is given a gentle slap on his wrist. Outside, in the white white world, his conviction in some cases is merely 'battle honours'. But this legal racial bias towards the white pigmentation explains the vindictive powerlessness of any British Race Relations law where blacks and Asians are concerned. Consequently, what we see happening in Britain today reinforces the aggression emitting from Asian, West Indian and African peoples; about the vindictiveness, through material greed, of Britain's violent and racist methods in the legal administration of those continents. The white British stormtrooper action towards Britain's non-white nationals, comes sizzling hot from her memory. For it is merely a reflection of Britannia's negative attitudes which she used to keep her colonial non-whites' Independence struggles within British perspectives. At that time she was doing what is known as 'taking care of business'. She was only treading water in the balance of time. On the streets of present-day Britain, in the hearts of black and Asian peoples, there are devastating moods; a community crawling with clues for quality time. It tastes like this. In the tearful world of 'capital competition', where 'winning and losing' is the name of the game. If you prefer to think that being an Imperial Colonizer means you have 'won', then the blatant truth is, since decolonization, Great Britain has been heavily engrossed in losing all the 'winnings'. She is now in a reactive rapid transfer stage, when governments with few answers usually end up saying: 'Let them eat cake'. Let them know this in Liverpool, Southall, Brixton, Bristol and anywhere else tragedy takes place.

I broke into numerous visions, when I noticed through the railings of a kindergarten, a multi-racial class of kids. Playing with life, never minding luck. They were gardening, sitting around discovering each other. In one corner of the garden, I perceived a group of three or four free souls, all holding Union Jacks with Prince Charles and Lady Diana stamped in the centre. For me, children are half a stretch away from imagination. In a way, it's promise-food for dream-box. It was a brightening scene and I felt good.

The importance of that scenario only hit home when a white kid, with resolve as per his size, grabbed the National Emblem out of the hand of his black friend. Watched by two others, a brown and a white, the black, all of four or five, put a spell on his ideas and snatched his property back. Turned on by his success, he began to run the changes, proudly waving his flag as his sign of victory. Gradually, with a little action from their teacher, peace returned to the play space.

Awareness flooded my thoughts. From that simple scene, I focused on Tomorrow. Transferring that child through the hustle of time, I placed him getting around a few years hence. I pondered a moment to get to the effect. I bounced a little with my thoughts. 'What,' I asked myself, 'if that child grows up to discover the Union Jack he was holding would one day stone him in the guts?' Or maybe, wouldn't even let him get up off the ground floor?

Feeling I was onto something, it wasn't time to mess around. I headed for some conniggeration, for other opinions. Later on that day, I breezed back home and began to think, constitutionally. If that child, in that not far off time, has only heard the insecurities of whites, with their personal axes constantly grinding it on his head, through the labels 'immigrants', 'repatriation', 'deportation' while still calling him the derogatory term, 'coloured', he will in less than half the time it takes to form a thought, be *another* rebel.

The reality is, in any of Britain's ex-colonies, white racial and material interests have always been safeguarded, by virtue of being an inherent part of the fabric of that society. Let us also remember that whites, in setting up the infrastructure of government, land ownership and commerce, in those then colonies, cunningly weaved themselves in, to become *the* structure itself. A racial sit-in. They belonged to everything, and every club there was, to keep an eye on things. They were *the* government, and owed allegiance to the British monarch. So did all the blacks and Asians. Her Majesty's 'subjects' they most certainly were, and 'British' in name only. Notice for Britain's black and Asian peoples, in the theory of being a 'British subject' the white British practice of citizenship, when applied to their colonized peoples, the practice always came first. *Subject to Britain,* was the order of the day. When Britannia needed compulsory volunteers to fight for 'King and Country', the use of her 'subjects' was a foregone conclusion. But in white Britain, after *her* danger was over, racial 'accidental amnesia' suddenly occurred. The only wartime contribution she 'suddenly' remembered reared up with a vengeance when Ian Smith announced a Unilateral Declaration of Independence. A national white British Spasm Band, sensing the spark of international cries, especially from black and Asian countries, for British military action, streaked into a weighty action and pumped into a black hide-beating refrain: 'kith and kin, kith and kin, they fought beside us during World War Two.' The heat was too much for a British government, who never had any intention of sending British troops to quell the white rebellion. Incidentally, the government did offer the Aldershot Regiment to Nigeria's Prime Minister, Sir Abubakar Tafawa Balewa, who was at almost the same moment undergoing a successful *coup d'état*. The Aldershot Regiment was placed on seventy-hour alert, but was never used, not having been requested by the Nigerians.

When Ian Smith and the white Rhodesian immigrants became

white Zimbabweans, the British government was most insistent on the protection of white lives and the racial interests of Zimbabwe's whites. And in order to give more foundation to white Zimbabwean interests, the Great White Father trumpeted in unison with those whites: how they had built the country, as usual with their bare hands, from nothing, forgetting that the black Zimbabweans performed *all* physical tasks. They now delivered what all of Africa's whites consider *their* killer-punch: 'the country will fall into rack and ruin without whites'. Those whites? There are others, who most probably possess far more integrity. Blacks in Zimbabwe and in Azania (South Africa), know very well that there is a fine line between black necessity for those particular whites and the destruction of blacks by those same whites.

Today, Zimbabwe, for a white minority with the help of Britain's government, protects the racial interests of Zimbabwe's whites. Who are also very much part of the fabric of state.

Black and Asian people have for several centuries contributed to the British economy; even more so than Zimbabwe's whites have done so for Zimbabwe. Significantly, countless black and Asian lives have either been butchered at the hands of Britain's whites, or lost in numerous wars fighting for Britain, especially World Wars One and Two. Why then, are their racial interests not being reflected in the social and political life of Britain? Is it because they cannot totally look like, speak like, or eat the same foods as the whites; in fact murder their own identity? The truth is, when Britain's whites arrived in *any* colony, they practised the same white-superior-implacable attitudes in others' territory. They kept themselves strictly apart, while making the local inhabitants house serfs. And those 'Gods on Earth' required an army of pathetically paid interpreters to make themselves understood, not being able to speak any of the languages. Most of those whites, who walked in boots of arrogance, even after twenty years' residency could still not speak the local language. Local citizens were made to learn English. Yet, in Britain, white cries of 'we can't understand what they are saying', or 'they have such thick accents', underlines a major hypocrisy, or those colonial whites kept the truth of their attitudes and their brutalities from those at home in Britain. However, black and Asian people, having suffered the self-same treatment from whites who have never even ventured out of this fair isle, can, with some justification, believe that racial injustice to be part of the white British body politic.

In times of crisis, previously, Her Majesty's Government announced 'we want you to fight in the coming war, the life of the Empire is threatened'. What the Great White Father meant was that white lives were threatened; so black lives must defend them and be sacrificed, if need be, in their defence. That Walt Disney-type idea of 'answering the call' will not work again, until the black and brown British community can visibly see what interest they have in the state of Great Britain. If they are part of the fabric of the state through its institutions, then they will possess a reason for allegiance. At this point in time, holding a racially-devaluing British passport means absolutely nothing. I would have thought it makes sense. Surely Britain's internal stability is paramount?

Consider this idea. What does the British government intend to do in the event of a military crisis, with an element in its population whose loyalty it is not sure of? Internment? Almost two million people? Or is there an ambitious scientific programme planned, in order to subdue a large amount of that population?

If the allegiance of British blacks and browns has already been decided, then keeping their parents out of the fabric of Britain's multi-racial(?) society, defeats the object. This is confession time, and the period for performing conjuring tricks is over. And so are cut-rate citizenships.

Imagination is useful, for those who have a use for it. There are some cut-rate word artists for whom imagination is a tedious stumbling block and reality a misconception. Therefore, their conception of reality stretches my imagination. Clean out of sight.

Will the rule of newspapers be the lie in our lives? Who will believe it? Why? Editor of *Race Today*, Darcus Howe, has for years been speaking out about the reality of life in Brixton for blacks and Asian people. This has earned him the static label 'Race Leader' from the artistic race word-weavers of the balanced-bias-towards-white press. The abundance of this style of reporting suggests that these thinkers have the same thoughts, which again suggests sheep who also move in the same direction when the thoughts of their identity is in racial crisis. But we need the press to be significantly free, in order to guarantee *all* of our freedoms, liberty, and freedom of speech. The black and Asian community is also an integral part of the British community and also requires those journalists to use equality for their nib. Therefore, why have those race reporters failed to put the boot into the race leaders of the House of Commons, who *are* race leaders in the strictest sense? They represent the interest of only one race. Thus cutting another large chunk out of the quality time of those other British people, who happen to have a different colour of skin. So what happens to the 'Special relationship' of the white, brown and black British people?

Nevertheless, that 'Special relationship' is a bring-down. For a moment, just for a moment, six years ago, the black community thought that it had a positive commitment from a British institution. The British Broadcasting Corporation. It lasted a moment. Paranoia, being a series of unacceptable possibilities, came heavily into play. There was the possibility that 'Black Londoners', presented by Alex Pascal, might be a success. The programme, to be heard five days a week with a captive audience of Londoners reflecting a black British view, quickly became unacceptable – that is, financially. Surely, a programme which reflects the views of the other Britain should be considered a priority for real financial backing? Or are there so many programmes reflecting black views all over Britain that 'Black Londoners' is not considered a paramount social investment? And the possibility of the black and brown community having a stake in state institutions fades away into star-dust. Is 'Black Londoners' an SOG? Save Our Guilt.

They're building rainbows in the white-house tonight. At the Commission for Racial Equality the corridors are full of hunters helping the hunted. To give answers to questions, through no understanding, desks full of assumptions, the community asks 'What do we do now? You are our racial valium.' They tread water in vain, without thinking why they are no nearer the hues and shades that brought them to fruition, for they know that the future of the other Britain is also the decider of social stability. Have you ever tried walking a tight-rope a million miles in the air knowing whatever happens, you must only come down on one side?

The attitude of Britain's black and brown people to the CRE is conclusively reflected in an article of the *Caribbean Times,* in July 1981:

Equal Opportunities

The single biggest disaster area of the CRE's activities has been the failure of its white dominated Equal Opportunities Division (EOD) headed by Ex-Colonial Peter Sanders, to make headway in their formal investigations in eliminating racial discrimination, despite the massive powers given to it by Parliament and the generous resources allocated to it in terms of staff and access to outside lawyers.

After four years, only ten puny investigations have been completed.

Employment

In *Employment,* the most important area affecting blacks, not a single major investigation has been completed nor is likely to be completed in the foreseeable future. The E.O.D. is reluctant to take on the Civil Service or the powerful professions.

E.S.N.

NOT a single education investigation has been completed! Nothing has been done about the disadvantage suffered by black kids as a result of racial stereotyping on the part of education authorities and teachers, which so seriously undermines the future of whole generations of blacks. Not a single investigation has been completed into the educational policies and teacher attitudes which condemn black kids to the school dustbins of remedial classes and their categorization as educationally sub normal.

Advertisements

THE reluctance of Sanders and his investigators to act decisively and effectively in using the law to confront discriminators is best illustrated by the manner in which they take great pains to avoid taking our legal proceedings against those who place racially discriminatory advertisements.

In 1980, the CRE 'disposed of' 32 advertisement complaints.

18 were found to be unlawful, but they were all settled *informally*!

When fear knocks on the door, a stranger on the other side is not necessarily a saviour. The CRE has up till now few saving graces. It has failed to become an organization all races have confidence in. If the nation needs agents of balm, so be it. But it is clearly obvious that the black and brown communities have no confidence in the personnel of the CRE.

The directed task for the CRE of creating racial stability based on white race assumptions of non-whites, is impossible. The possibility of confidence in the CRE coupled with equal representation of all races has been made impossible because the race conflict within it gives even less confidence to the black and brown communities. The possibility that the CRE began with an assumed misconception of Britain's blacks and Asians dismisses it.

If this fang-less institution is to gather any heavy momentum, then why has it not begun hide-beating all authorities who possess every single historical document on black and Asian history to be housed in its own archives, e.g. records of the slave trade, colonial history, all contributions of black and Asian people in all wars fought for Britain in order that all the British people are given the benefit of historical research.

Voltaire clarifies what can be considered to be the black and Asian dilemma about British history. So, what is seduced into the skulls of school pupils is highly questionable. He wrote:

The Certainty of History

Any certainty which is not mathematical demonstration is only extreme probability: this is all that historical certainty can ever be.

Marco Polo was the first and at that time the only person to speak of the greatness and of the population of China; he was not believed and he could not expect to be believed. The Portuguese, who entered this vast empire several centuries later, made its existence probable. It is now certain, with that certainty which arises from the unanimous testimony of a thousand eyewitnesses of different nations when this testimony is challenged by no one.

Using Voltaire's thoughts, therefore, Britain's history to Britain's whites is a certainty. To European countries in the family affair of white oppression of the world's non-white peoples, it is also a certainty. To those whites who have no other source, it is only possibly true. For the thoughtless, it is extreme probability. But to those non-white peoples of the world, it is extremely probable that British history is a cover-up, based on an extreme certainty, that *any* cover-up of *any* oppression is a camouflage for mendacities. So what is the truth of British history?

Moreover, the CRE makes the scene by what it has not done. The pathetic myths still perpetuated about non-white peoples are damaging to the social and intellectual structure of Britain, and this does not seem to be too high on its list of conference-going activities.

It's on the beam. Without a doubt the great British youth shall inherit the mistakes of the (mis) leaders, who load up and make tracks for better horizons when the going gets tough. They leave behind them the same magical statements to give courage and optimism to British youth: 'greater productivity', 'fewer strikes', and 'more efficiency'; meaningless phrases conjured up, out of sight, back in historical time. They have listened to the droppings of the paper party men and women. How can Britain's youth relate to leaders who are an experience and two classes removed? They have every reason to rebel, with no jobs, no prospects but a guaranteed place in the great British dole queue. Today, they have witnessed a defiance in black and brown youth and they are allies. The ethic of white superiority means nothing. They see action, they see refusal, and a future for refusal. A unification of the victimized is twice as bad in retaliation.

I have a young white friend, Nathaniel McBride, he is ten years old. Recently, his homework studies required him to write a project/critique on 'Stanley finds Livingstone' from *The True Book of Great Adventures,* published in 1978. He wrote:

As I have been writing about David Livingstone for my school project I would like to critize a few things about the book I was working from. I. For my first criticism I shall quote from the book. All words and sentences underlined show that they are either ridicule and impossible or that they are trying to make out that whites are superior to blacks.

'In 1844 a group of *frightened* natives implored Livingstone to drive off a savage lion that was attacking their sheep. Livingstone wounded the lion with his first shot, but before he could fire the second barrel, the enraged animal pounced on him and shook him like a terrier shakes a rat. Lying helpless on the ground, Livingstone was mauled by the lion *for several minutes*. His life was saved by an elderly African named Mebalwe, who reloaded the gun and fired. He missed the animal which promptly savaged both him and a native, before finally dropping dead as a result of the first shot.'

The first underlined word is 'Frightened', the reason for this is that I myself do not think a tribe of natives, whose fathers had been living in the jungle for thousands and thousands of years, would be frightened of a lion and would ask a European who knows nothing about lions to kill one. The second underlining is also unlikely. I wonder if there really was a lion.

This young opinion makes the scene for the changing face of Britain. It shows that each generation is one more moment removed from the traditions that can hold a nation back.

The past is a dead living entity to be perceived from totally honest objectivity. Youth is placed in a better position to do just that.

The answer was stamped on brown faces reclining, who weathered storm deaths, as their Time stood the test. Remember New Cross and Southall's burning surprises, and the history of white still remained covered yet wet; there's a time for reflection and a time for regret; a time when race violence, may not be over just yet. But the answers will stand firm, their future is cast; the Great British People, viewed again their Question, looked into their colonial past, stared twice at the future, as *their* answer came out at last . . .

The presence of the black and brown British people must be
THE ANSWER.